The
New Calvinism
Considered

Jeremy Walker

EP BOOKS
Faverdale North
Darlington
DL3 oPH, England

web: http://www.epbooks.org

e-mail: sales@epbooks.org

EP Books are distributed in the USA by:
JPL Distribution
3741 Linden Avenue Southeast
Grand Rapids, MI 49548
E-mail: orders@jpldistribution.com
Tel: 877.683.6935

British Library Cataloguing in Publication Data available

ISBN 978–0–85234–968–7

The new Calvinism is proving to be such an influence on the global Christian church that it is now impossible to ignore it. But what are we to make of it? Jeremy Walker's evaluation is brief, informed, discerning and fair. Best of all, it is filled with grace as well as truth. Those who read it will be heartened by its encouragements and sobered by its warnings. Those who are wise will take its message to heart.

Stuart Olyott, *pastor, missionary and author*

Someone needed to write an evaluation of the new Calvinism of the "young, restless, and Reformed." And it certainly had to be someone younger than me! Thank God for (young) Jeremy Walker's able assessment of this massive movement. The new Calvinism provokes either joy or fear (and perhaps some of both) in many depending on what part of it one has experienced and one's reaction to it.

The best thing about this assessment is that Jeremy has approached the matter in genuinely Christian fashion. He speaks of the difficulty of speaking accurately about such a large and diverse movement. He understands the necessity of guarding his criticisms in a way that is deeply Christian. He does not forget to commend the movement where it can and ought to be commended. Nevertheless the critique he launches loses none of its helpfulness and power for all this. He notes how difficult it is boldly to provide such criticisms in the context of the cult of celebrity and triumphalism that sometimes characterizes the New Calvinism. It is always difficult to be the little boy who tells the world that the emperor has no clothes (or has at least stripped down to his underwear), but Jeremy does so with both candor and kindness.

Jeremy is careful not to paint with brush-strokes that stain the portraits of the innocent. He, however, provides a wide-ranging critique. He kindly but incisively speaks of its tendency to *triumphalism*, the divide within it over Charismatic views of the *spiritual gifts*, its embracing some with a dangerously broad *ecumenism*, its important and deep disagreements over matters of *holiness* (the place of works in sanctification and antinomianism), its deeply questionable Kuyperian views of *culture* with their tendency to destroy the distinction between the holy and the profane, and its ugly tendency to embrace *pragmatism and commercialism* in church life.

If you are not sure what to think of the new Calvinism, you need to read this book. If you have friends struggling with it, you need to give them this book. If you are being reproached for not embracing it, use the arguments and cautions of this book to defend yourself. If you are in danger of rejecting the whole of new Calvinism root and branch, you need the care of this book to restrain you. My prayer is that God will give this little book great usefulness!

Dr Sam Waldron, *Academic Dean of the Midwest Center for Theological Studies*

As the young, restless and reformed movement(s) appears to be slowly but surely running its course, the big question is: what has it provided that is of lasting value, for which we should be grateful, and where has it fallen short of expectations and, indeed, of biblical orthodoxy? This short booklet by Jeremy Walker seeks to address these questions in a manner that is both irenic and critical. A very useful contribution to the literature on the subject.

Carl Trueman, *Professor of Historical Theology and Church History holding the Paul Woolley Chair of Church History at Westminster Theological Seminary, Philadelphia*

The new Calvinism is a fairly recent phenomenon and a rather nebulous movement still in flux—not an easy subject for analysis and critique. Is this truly a resurgence of biblical and Calvinist conviction, or is it just the latest evangelical fad—a new decoration on the sputtering pragmatist bandwagon? Jeremy Walker has made a thoughtful, instructive, even-handed assessment of the most visible and influential streams of the new Calvinism. He acknowledges aspects of the movement that are encouraging and beneficial, but he also points out and carefully critiques several deeply troubling tendencies. The result is a perceptive and profitable appraisal of a complex, sometimes confusing, trend among young evangelicals—and a clear signpost pointing the right way ahead for a movement now at the crossroads.

Phil Johnson, *Executive Director at* Grace to You

We are all caught up in movements of religious thought, and at the current time none is more pervasive than the movement known as the 'New Calvinism'. Some of its leading figures have become celebrities of evangelicalism; many of its leading ideas—drawn in the most part from Reformed thinkers—have impacted church life in a variety of ways. In this book, Jeremy Walker helps both to introduce the movement to us, and to weigh up some of its characteristics. This is a helpful guide, appreciative with discernment, and critical without condemnation. Its conclusion is deceptively simple: we must be Reformed—that is, biblical—Christians, and we must be ourselves. Jeremy's engagement will help us to 'try the spirits' and to live and minister in a biblical, God-honouring way.

Rev. Dr Iain D Campbell, *Free Church of Scotland, Point, Isle of Lewis*

Contents

Preface

Several years ago I wrote a brief piece on the new Calvinism on a personal blog called *The Wanderer*. It garnered more attention and stimulated more discussion than many other articles. On the back of that effort, I was asked by a church in the US if I would be prepared to deal with the topic in an adult Sunday School class. I semi-willingly agreed. That material also proved popular, and was transcribed, edited and made available in a number of formats online. A number of friends found it useful or engaged with it in some way. I also treated the topic at some length in an adult Sunday School class in the congregation which I serve. Several members had been influenced by or exposed to the new Calvinism, either having appreciated and benefited from some of its best features or been threatened and scarred by some of its worst.

Since then, without wishing to gain a reputation as 'the bloke who does new Calvinism,' still less as a man seeking to develop one of those 'discernment ministries' that seems to consist in little more than consistent and virulent attacks against anyone who differs one iota from him on any point of doctrine, I have had opportunities to present this material in other environments, and have subsequently received a number of encouragements to put it into print. Again, I do so with a measure of reluctance, because of the constantly changing manifestations of a movement still growing and developing, because I do not wish to be a mere controversialist, and because it is quite clear that this topic is one on which various true brothers in Christ feel very deeply.

That said, I trust that this material is timely, judicious, clear, reasonable and fair, and will help those within, without and around the movement currently described as new Calvinism to make some profitable assessments, accept some particular encouragements, take account of some specific challenges, and consider some genuine concerns. As will be explained and explored further below, new Calvinism is, in brief, the label applied to the resurgence of certain central aspects of Calvinistic doctrine within conservative evangelicalism, though it is usually associated with other convictions and actions that do not or may not immediately derive from the teaching and example of John Calvin and others of similar faith and life. Of necessity, the short book you are reading assumes a certain degree of knowledge about the movement and its key movers, but I hope that many of you will either have some sense of these things already or will be able to follow up the references. Where that is the case, I trust that most of the observations will appear self-evident. Where explanations seem required, I have attempted to offer them as briefly and clearly as possible.

My concern is to be faithful to God and subject to his truth, as well as faithful to the saints, whether in agreement or disagreement with them. I would rather use hard arguments than hard words. This little volume is therefore offered in the sincere and humble hope of it doing good to God's people and bringing glory to God.

Chapter 1
Comprehending the new Calvinism

Ifirst came across some of the men who are now known as new Calvinists a few years after John Piper first published *Desiring God* in 1986. A friend of mine was enthusing about the book and told me, 'You have to read this book, it will change your life.' I thought that if a friend was speaking of a book in this way then I should at least do him the honour of reading it. Since then I have been engaged with the new Calvinism in various ways. A number of my peers have been very much caught up with it, and I have felt the pressure to imbibe it, to embrace it, to be a part of it.

This interest and engagement has continued even

though this movement has sometimes seemed to be largely an American phenomenon. I therefore acknowledge that I have something of an outside perspective on those aspects of it. That said, it has become increasingly apparent that the stream flows both ways, and that there are mutual influences and echoes. Though at one point I thought that the new Calvinism in the UK lacked the breadth of the US approach, I have begun to see various manifestations of it in an increasing number of places. In the UK, though it may not always use the same labels, the concepts and concerns of the new Calvinism have their own expression, reflecting some of the same emphases and attitudes, differences and divisions as are found in the US, but having sometimes their own distinct flavour. So, for example, some of these elements are found in such diverse movements as the Newfrontiers churches or World Harvest Mission; others are more prevalent in groupings like the FIEC, Affinity and the Proclamation Trust; they come to light in initiatives like Gospel Partnerships and conferences like New Word Alive; certain personalities have particular influence in seminary circles. Of course, as in the US, there are overlaps between various groups.

Please note that I am not saying that all or any of these groups would formally or officially classify themselves as new Calvinists—something that, given the nature of the movement as discussed below, it would be hard to do. Rather, as one considers the elements of principle and practice that often coalesce in what is generally labelled as new Calvinism, those principles and practices, for better or worse, may be more rather than less evident in some of these circles. In this respect, it can be hard to provide 'documentary evidence' for the assertion that some individual or group is, in some measure, new Calvinist. Few deliberately self-identify using that label. Rather, one is considering common emphases, matters of tone and tenor. While this might seem rather nebulous, I hope that it will become clear that some of those common emphases can be identified, and that—where they are held and practiced as a whole—we are likely to be looking somewhere along the new Calvinist spectrum.

As I engaged with the new Calvinism I was stimulated by and often appreciated much of what I read and heard and saw. I benefited from some of it, sometimes greatly, and disagreed with some of it, sometimes vigorously. That is still the case. The process of evaluation has been (and remains) a long one in which reading, listening, discussing, and attending conferences all play a part.

Any survey and assessment of this order is admittedly like a snapshot of a recently discovered animal: just when you think you have captured the essence of the creature it moves again and you discover something new. As such, a final or conclusive assessment is not immediately possible. That said, I have found that while the nuances of this critique have necessarily developed, its broad strokes have remained fairly constant. Despite these continuing developments, the new Calvinism has been for some short time a fairly significant movement within Western evangelicalism, especially of the variety which calls itself Reformed, which is one of the reasons behind the largely unabated pressure to jump on the bandwagon. However, while I hope that no true-hearted saint would wish to dismiss what is profitable, none of us can thoughtlessly embrace this or anything else without careful consideration.

It is out of that tension and that developed process that I hope to bring some observations, writing as a Christian, as a pastor and as part of a generation that has seen the new Calvinism take off and take hold over a period of years. You may, perhaps, be wondering if this is relevant to you. It may be that the names, sermons, books, conferences, and issues addressed in this material seem fairly remote from you. Indeed, they may be. However, for many men and women in Reformed circles—whether in churches, seminaries, associations and affiliations formal or otherwise—these very names, sermons, books, conferences and issues are the ones now being endorsed, heard, read, attended and absorbed, and which are having a formative, even determinative, influence upon many, especially among the young. For some, this may all seem immediately relevant, and you are plunging into a world that you know intimately. Others may be somewhere in between. I hope that I can provide all readers with fair and judicious insights that may be of help in understanding and, as appropriate, responding to these things.

Before proceeding, however, I want to issue some *caveats*, some initial warnings which we must take into account as we look at the new Calvinism.

The nature of the assessment

First of all, this is *a personal and pastoral assessment*. I am not pretending that I have a monopoly on insights into individual men and the movement as a whole, or that I speak a final and infallible word on the matter. I may be mistaken in what I suggest. There are thousands of blog posts and books and videos and conferences with which I have had no interaction or engagement. The very speed of development means that it is hard to be complete, and every time I seek to consider these things I am again prompted to what I hope are fresher and more accurate understandings and a deeper awareness of the issues. If I am ignorant, mistaken, or misguided at any point, I hope I am prepared to be instructed or corrected and thus to fine tune my understanding.

The spirit of the assessment

Secondly, I am seeking to provide *a balanced and appropriately irenic appreciation*. I am not dealing with those I have already concluded to be—altogether and without exception—lunatics or heretics, and so I am not setting out to address them as would be appropriate under such circumstances. Neither do I intend to lay waste to everything that is before me (even where I disagree). I have several friends who would call themselves new Calvinists, friends whom I respect and appreciate, and with some of whom I feel able readily to cooperate as opportunity provides. I am by no means seeking to dismiss these friends or to trample them into the dust. Where some of this material has been made available previously in the public sphere, I have been condemned for using fraternal language of the new Calvinists of any and every stripe. Such condemnations suggest that the new Calvinists ought not to be considered as brothers and should not be spoken of as such. As we shall see, such a blanket condemnation is neither righteous nor gracious. Though I might disagree on several matters, have profound concerns in some areas, and be persuaded of certain great dangers, I am in no doubt that I am generally dealing with genuine brothers and sisters in Christ, not all of whom embrace the principles or practices about which I am more generally concerned. While there are some who call themselves new Calvinists who are meddling with orthodox faith and life, it would be entirely unfair to tar all with the same brush. We need an intelligent and thoughtful and Scriptural perspective, and to judge each case on its own merits or lack of them.

At the same time, for reasons that are set out below, I have no hesitation in affirming that it is not right to deal in a brotherly fashion with some who are increasingly dabbling with a Christianity that is not merely on the fringes of the historic stream of orthodox faith but has pushed outside the envelope. So, while I have a desire for genuine understanding, true unity and gospel peace, we must remember that unity and peace at the expense of truth and righteousness is a wicked trade-off. Nevertheless, a gentle and gracious approach is not the same as an endorsement of error, and is entirely consistent with a vigorously-held and ardently-promoted orthodoxy (see 2 Timothy 2:24–26).

This assessment, then, is not intended to be a hatchet job. There is a great danger in becoming a professional cynic, or at the very least a perpetual sceptic or an inveterate critic. I do not wish to give vent to a sarcastic strain, nor fall into the trap of painting a caricature of new Calvinism that could easily be mocked. Such a straw man is tempting to erect precisely because it is easier to knock down than the real thing. I should also point out that though writing unashamedly as a persuaded confessional, Particular Baptist, I am not setting out to accomplish a sort of Reformed and/or Baptist whitewash. This is not an exercise in which, on my own behalf or that of others, I seek to climb above others, confident in a certain universal superiority, smugly suggesting that if only everyone were more like me or us, this world would be a better place. It is not my intention mindlessly to ignore, defend or attack any particular group, but to deal fairly with the new Calvinism. Please understand this, especially when I (of necessity) use the language of 'them' and 'us'.

The object of the assessment

The third and the most important caveat is that *the new Calvinism is not monolithic.* It is not a single and uniform entity. As we have already been suggesting above, the new Calvinism is a spectrum. It is a broad river with many currents, having different eddies with varying depths and shallows. Furthermore, the principle that those who shout loudest are often most readily heard may hold good here. There are a number of prominent and vocal characters, some of them talented self-promoters or ably promoted by others, who have gained or manufactured a highly visible platform. They are not always spokesmen for the group as a whole, though they may at times seem to be.

All this is especially important to remember in

considering both the commendations and the critiques
that follow. It is the main reason why we cannot zero
in on a narrow part of the spectrum and then declare
universal approbation or universal condemnation on all
who are at any point along that same spectrum, however
distant from the point of immediate consideration.
Some who have assessed the new Calvinism have been
swift to damn it all and everyone in any association with
it; others defend it uniformly, endorsing everything and
everyone. Neither approach is wise or fair. We must
bear in mind that not all those who call themselves
(or are called by others) new Calvinists are entitled to
all the commendations or subject to all the criticisms
that follow, nor are they all formally connected with
each other. Some will receive both commendation and
criticism, in some cases the cautions and criticisms
necessarily compromising the commendations to some
degree.

Again, we must take account of the fact that some
have taken the name new Calvinism, and others have
had the name thrust upon them. It is important to note
that there are degrees of association in this movement,
and—working along the spectrum and through the
various groupings—there are some who would fight shy
of any sort of formal union or cooperation with certain
others, and so, again, we must be wary of assuming that
this is some great and absolute theological or religious

bloc that stands and falls together. It would not be fair, for example, to assume that every ship from the new Calvinist shipyard sails under the same flag, and so either to attack, ignore or to salute them all on that basis.

This is one reason for my care in making the assertions that I do. Please also take into account that in an assessment such as this I have necessarily to paint with a broad brush, not having the opportunity to nuance and finesse some of my comments. Individuals considered in the light of my observations should be assessed as to whether or not, or at what points and to what degree, they fit the template. Exceptions to some of my general statements could easily be found. I understand that this is the case, but I am obliged to deal in generalities to some extent, recognizing that there will be exceptions. I will have to refer to points on a spectrum, but I do not mean to imply that all these things are universal or uniform when they are not.

Chapter 2
Characteristics of
the new Calvinism

Although we have already sounded the briefest note as to the nature of the new Calvinism, we need to explain more fully, as well as carefully and fairly, what it is that we are considering. What are the qualities of the new Calvinism? How do you define this movement, taking into account that it is a spectrum? Where do you start?

Calvinism

The first—and perhaps somewhat obvious quality—is *Calvinism* itself, though even this must be qualified. In general, this movement is united by convictions about the sovereignty of God in salvation, hence the name 'new Calvinists.' Note, however, that an appreciation of God's sovereignty in salvation is not necessarily the same thing as being 'Calvinistic' or 'Reformed.' Those labels have referents that are both historical and spiritual, both of which are much debated from every side. Perhaps one of the more insightful and heart-warming definitions of Calvinism comes from B. B. Warfield in his essay on this topic, where he states that the essence of the thing lies 'in a profound apprehension of God in His majesty, with the inevitably accompanying poignant realization of the exact nature of the relation sustained to Him by the creature as such, and particularly by the sinful creature ... when the sinful soul rests in humble, self-emptying trust purely on the God of grace.'[1]

However, while there is a very real sense in which Calvinism is more than just the five points,[2] it is not so easy to argue that it is less than those points. Here we must take into account that not all the new Calvinists are, in fact, Calvinists. Some are what are called Amyraldians. Moïse (or Moses) Amyraut was a French theologian who developed what was basically a 'four point' (or four-and-a-half point) semi-Calvinism. The primary issue of contention is the nature and extent of the atonement. Several within the new Calvinist movement believe in what is sometimes described as 'unlimited limited atonement'—the idea that the death of Jesus was intended for all men but that it is effectively applied only to the elect. (By contrast, the classical Calvinist's conviction would be that the death of Jesus was intended only for the elect and therefore did not fail or fall short in any point or degree.)[3] Taking all this into account, we must admit that the title of the well-known book by Collin Hansen which has become almost a label for the movement, *Young, Restless, Reformed*, is much catchier than *Young, Restless and mainly Calvinistic, apart from those of us who are basically Amyraldian.* Nevertheless, for the sake of simplicity, I will continue to use the phrase 'new Calvinism' to describe this movement.

This movement can be described (slightly inaccurately) as Calvinistic insofar as it maintains a general unity around the notion that God is sovereign in the salvation of sinners. However, in a further twist, one could argue that the true father figure of the new Calvinism is probably more Jonathan Edwards than John Calvin, and even then it is Jonathan Edwards mediated through John Piper. This is significant, not just because of the genuine debates over Edwards' legacy from outside the movement, but because of the selective way in which Edwards is often presented. I am not suggesting that Piper is a negligible Edwards scholar, nor do I wish to give the impression that I have read more of Edwards or understand him better than John Piper (who I am sure would wish others to go away and read Edwards for themselves). However, I hope that I have read enough of Edwards to say that the Edwards of the new Calvinists is not the full-orbed Edwards of even the two volume edition of his works, let alone the complete scholarly corpus. There is much more to Edwards, even at his most readily available, than a sort of patron saint of Christian hedonism. And yet it is this rather narrow and imbalanced version of Edwards that is the popular conception not just of Edwardseanism (if you will forgive the awkwardness) but of Calvinism itself among many of the new Calvinists, so much so that sometimes this is the lens through which Edwards' theology and much else is now read and interpreted.

Characters

Secondly, this is a movement of *characters* (or figureheads, personalities, celebrities or gurus, depending on how pejorative a label you wish to apply, or what kind of a follower you are dealing with). If you spend enough time in this environment you might eventually theorize that there is somewhere an inner sanctum where these magisterial figures sit, the controllers of what has been referred to, tongue-in-cheek, as the Evangelical Industrial Complex. These are the men who appear on the key websites, videoed in cool monochrome sitting around discussing great principles and actions and movements while others sit in humble awe as they deliver their weighty opinions. I do not say that this is how all these men perceive themselves, but it is clearly how they are perceived by certain others, and it is a perception that some seem happy to permit or foster. Often these are established figures, the big names who need to be at the conferences in order for them to be real new Calvinist conferences. Alongside them are the rising stars of the upcoming generation.

At the core you will hear names such as John Piper, Mark Dever, C. J. Mahaney, Al Mohler, Mark Driscoll, Matt Chandler, Kevin DeYoung, Ligon Duncan, Tim Keller, Don Carson, and Wayne Grudem. On the websites and in the blogosphere names like Justin Taylor and Tim Challies are prominent.

More on the fringes, and with a much more ambivalent relationship, are men like R. C. Sproul Sr. and John MacArthur on the one hand and James MacDonald and Francis Chan on the other. I mention these names not to suggest that they are birds of a feather but because they are points of reference and interaction within the movement and have often strong connections within it, and sometimes sit around the same tables (for example, Sproul and MacArthur have both made regular appearances at the Together for the Gospel conference, a biennial pastors' conference whose instigators are Ligon Duncan, Mark Dever, Albert Mohler, and C. J. Mahaney, each one part of the new Calvinist sphere). However, men like Sproul and MacArthur do not fit readily into the spectrum, either in their own reckoning or that of others. The relationship is more tense, sometimes involving mutual expressions of appreciation and sometimes critiques and concerns. In the case of John MacArthur especially, those concerns and critiques have been increasingly blunt.[4] It is also worth noting that some of those who have become prominent for their interaction with the new Calvinism are often presumed to be alongside, if not within, the movement because they are 'part of the conversation'—perhaps someone like Voddie Baucham might fit into this category?

When you enter the world of the new Calvinism it is these core names that you will find in almost every place being heard, read or discussed. For example, in the online realm you will find that the hundreds if not thousands of new Calvinistic blogs are rehashing the same videos, passing on the same references, locked in a potentially nepotistic world of self-reference. Indeed, this feature makes it virtually impossible to engage the new Calvinists without 'naming names'—it is a movement built around names, and reference to them is unavoidable. It is almost impossible to assess the teaching without discussing the teachers. Generally speaking, I would rather deal with the issues, but the issues are so intertwined with the personalities that they are often inseparable. Furthermore, I have often been pressed to give examples and instances of the assertions I make. I have therefore attempted to do so, not with the intention of isolating and assaulting particular individuals, but as a means of identifying representative cases which demonstrate a measure of validity to the suggestions and contentions you will find here.

Do not misunderstand me: I recognise that God in his sovereignty can work through anyone and anything that he chooses. I also recognise that the Lord is pleased, at particular times, to raise up men of distinctive character and gift through whom he chooses to work in a more public or prominent way (and that other men of equally distinctive character and gift never attain to the same prominence). However, when we begin to yoke God's works necessarily to particular ones of his servants, we begin to tread on dangerous ground. The cult of celebrity in the modern West has infiltrated the church, so much so that we can seem to be presuming that the Lord is obliged to work or invariably will work when the right person or persons are present: get someone prominent to preach and people are bound to listen! But this is to forget, if not to ignore, the fact that the Lord is not bound in this way. Various groups and organisations face particular and sustained pressure, often though not always from younger believers (and sometimes with the implied suggestion that if these demands are not met, then they may take themselves and their custom elsewhere), to get the biggest names to the major events. All too often there is mere capitulation at this point, a failure to ask what these man stand for, what they carry with them by way of endorsement or conviction (even if not openly stated in a particular environment) and—sometimes at least as importantly—what they will open the door to by way of association. And, while I am not suggesting that it lies in precisely the same category of importance, the apostle of love himself recognises that there is such a thing as guilt by association: 'If anyone comes to you and does not bring this doctrine, do not receive him into your house nor greet him; for he who greets him shares in his evil deeds' (2 John 1:10–11). To return to the earlier illustration, if ships from the same shipyard do gather under the same flag, it is appropriate to assume that there is more than a hint of common ground and conviction, mutual appreciation and affection.

All this leads to at least three related dangers: the danger of slavish capitulation, the danger of mere imitation and the danger of unintended disconnection. Concerning the first, it is all too easy to suspend our own rational faculties when a word is perceived to have been spoken *ex cathedra*, wherever that seat of power may be. Christians in any circles readily go beyond the respect which ought to be legitimately afforded to proven men and become nothing more than children led away dancing to the piper's tune: then the 'top men' mentality can readily develop, in which 'ordinary Christians' or 'ordinary pastors' are content neither to think nor to act because they are being assured that the 'top men' have it all under control, and are thinking and acting for them. It is not uncommon to face what might be described as 'the argument from intelligence' which runs something like this: 'You have just disagreed with Piper/Grudem/Keller/Carson/scholar of choice. Do you know that this man has a brain the size of Belgium? You are clearly less intelligent and less well qualified than a man with more letters after his name than the average university faculty, and therefore you are not competent to have any disagreement with him nor are you capable of shifting my confidence in him.' This is not the fault of the scholarly men, but it is not good reasoning whether the name we are defending is a new Calvinist or something else. Such influence is especially significant where men with or without academic credentials are being touted or followed in seminaries. Friends who lecture or are otherwise involved with various seminaries in the UK assure me that the primary reading matter of the young men passing through these institutions, and the significant influences upon them in terms of principle and practice, faith and life, are the Kellers, Pipers and Carsons, and it is weight of personality and prominence that is the most telling thing with these would-be pastors and preachers. Here it is worth pondering the principle highlighted by J. Gresham Machen in his 1912 opening address on 'Christianity and Culture' at Princeton Seminary: 'What is today a matter of academic speculation begins tomorrow to move armies and pull down empires.' Without wishing to suggest that the men highlighted above are invariably unsafe guides or have nothing of real value to offer—quite the contrary, in some instances—it is worthwhile considering that they are having a significant influence on forming the next generation of leaders, who will themselves have an influence for better or for worse on many churches in coming days.

That brings us to the danger of mere imitation. Early in his life Andrew Fuller—who was to become a pre-eminent Particular Baptist theologian—discovered that the mark of a master ploughman was to be able to plough a straight line across the ridges of a field. Fuller assumed that such a standard could easily be achieved simply by laying your plough alongside an existing furrow created by a master and following it. Putting his theory to the test, he took a plough and went along the straight line of the master ploughman. When he had finished he looked back to see that although there was a degree of straightness because of the model that he followed, he had also copied and exaggerated all the kinks in the master ploughman's furrow. 'On perceiving this,' said Fuller, 'I threw the plough aside, and determined *never to be an imitator*.'5 The danger of these figureheads is that, in the minds of some, they become celebrities and gurus, perhaps even idols. Slavishly following them, their disciples reproduce not only much of what is good but also exaggerate them at their points of weakness or aberration. The same spirit is seen in the fact that many churches seem to operate under the conviction that they have seen the future, and it works: some congregations seem mindlessly to ape the approaches of the most prominent churches, as if the simple reproduction of their practices will secure the same ends. While this may in measure be true (do the same thing in the same kind of place and the same results may follow), even the movement's own principles of contextualization would seem to suggest that mere ecclesiastical mimicry is unhelpful. Why, then, can we go from place to place and find carbon copies of 'successful' churches springing up in different environments? That is not thoughtful adaptation but slavish emulation.

Furthermore, there is the danger of unintended

disconnection: as we consider some of these followers we find that there is a separation between men at the top of the hierarchy—often men of profound mental and emotional depth, who seek to hold unusual things (and sometimes, in the opinion of others, things that are contradictory or plain wrong) in tension in their thinking and practice—and those lower down the tree with, perhaps, less vision and capacity. A struggle follows, often issuing in a failure to hold those potentially fruitful or perhaps implicitly contradictory tensions. One or the other side must govern, leading to deviations from the doctrine and practice of the greater man by those of lesser magnitude. In other words, and as we shall see, some of what is happening at grass-roots level can be very far and very unhealthily removed from what is being proposed and modelled at the top. In some cases the apple is falling a fair distance from the tree and then rolling some way too. We might also note that this 'tribe of chiefs' mentality—and the language of tribalism is quite explicit in the new Calvinism—seems to be producing some significant tensions and is likely to produce more, especially as the disciples exaggerate or depart from certain emphases of the masters. Even those who explicitly ground their felt and expressed unity in a certain definition of the gospel—'I am of Christ'?—need to heed the warnings of 1 Corinthians 1:10–17.

It must be pointed out that, as yet, the UK has not really provided any champions of the new Calvinism of the same prominence as some on the American scene. This may be a matter of national character or simply the absence of candidates. I do not say that the British are incapable of hero-worship or elevating an individual, but I think that there is at present a greater scepticism in the UK, for better and for worse. That said, a few names have come to the fore. Several of the significant names come from within Newfrontiers — Terry Virgo, Tope Koleoso, and Adrian Warnock on the blogging front—though often by association with or commendation from the big cheeses from across the water. However, more recently, others like Steve Timmis and Tim Chester of the Crowded House and the Porterbrook Network have become more visible, in part because of Steve Timmis' role as the Director of the European chapter of the Acts 29 church planting movement. At the time of writing, the Porterbrook Network and Acts 29 have both become more closely involved with the Wales Evangelical School of Theology (WEST), where Jonathan Stephen has had some notable influence in directions that have much in common with new Calvinism.[6] Within the FIEC, there are several prominent individuals sounding the same notes, and the same is true within Affinity—again, while there may be no explicit embrace of the label of new

Calvinism, common themes, emphases, individuals and associations suggest the links. Evangelical Anglicanism has also been able to bask a little in the reflected glow of some of the more prominent American preachers and thinkers and there has been a measure of cross-fertilisation. One rule-of-thumb measure of prominence and engagement may be to see who from Britain receives the endorsement of the American scene, whether as conference speakers and preachers, bloggers, authors, or partners, or to which organisations and in which events the American side affiliates and becomes involved.

Conglomeration

Thirdly, this is a movement marked by *conglomeration*. It is a movement of coalitions, of conferences, of networks, and of networks of networks, numbers of men and churches operating together. As mentioned before, this can seem a little introspective at times (not that they are the only ones guilty of that): they all endorse one another's books and DVDs, they all refer to one another's blogs and videos. Together For The Gospel (T4G) and The Gospel Coalition (TGC) are two of the big overarching events or organizations holding some of these things together. In addition, there are such groups as the Acts 29 Network, Sovereign Grace Ministries, or the Resolved conference series. It is a broad and somewhat eclectic mix, reinforcing the idea of the spectrum and underlining the pursuit of a broad unity. (Again, I am not suggesting that everyone is sailing under the same flag, simply that there is a tendency for ships from this particular shipyard to gather together in convoys, bound by certain common aspirations and convictions. We should allow each ship to state and display its affiliations before reaching—and certainly before jumping to—any conclusions.)

Here, our noticing certain names of increasing prominence in the British arena allows us to see a similar developing scene here in the UK. Again, we look for common ground in terms of matters discussed, principles embraced, practices pursued, issues dismissed as irrelevant or elevated to the level of shibboleth. The recent marriage between WEST and Porterbrook (and, by extension, Acts 29) would be a case in point. I would suggest that the reorganisation and spreading influence of the FIEC, not least in its growing relationship with movements like Newfrontiers, manifests a readiness to learn from and emulate some of these American models. The broad reach of Affinity, with its general approach and objects of interest, suggests something that might quite like to become The British Gospel Coalition. Gospel Partnerships between free church and Anglican brothers have also received transatlantic endorsement and investment, and showcase the kind of coordination that is becoming more typical.

Let me be clear: though committed to the independence of local churches, I am equally committed to communion among churches. The confession of faith to which I subscribe quotes Ephesians 6:18, Psalm 122:6, Romans 16:1–2 and 3 John 8–10 to persuade us that

> As each church, and all the members of it, are bound to pray continually for the good and prosperity of all the churches of Christ, in all places, and upon all occasions to further every one within the bounds of their places and callings, in the exercise of their gifts and graces, so the churches, when planted by the providence of God, so as they may enjoy opportunity and advantage for it, ought to hold communion among themselves, for their peace, increase of love, and mutual edification.[7]

As such, the church which I serve enjoys close and fruitful relationships with like-minded congregations—across various groups and denominations—within and beyond the UK, and I appreciate personal friendships with men with whom I share much in terms of conviction and practice from a similar range. I think that the Scriptures command and commend a proper measure of cooperation among churches, and allow for me individually to pursue and enjoy good, deep and profitable personal friendships with faithful brothers from any strand or denomination of orthodox Christianity (indeed, I find that a measure of doctrinal clarity and conviction on both sides tends to enhance the friendship rather than damage it, because both parties know where they stand, and just how much and how profoundly they agree with one another).

However, while we will explore more fully some of the effects of this later on, the new Calvinist drive for conglomeration can introduce a degree of confusion. While many of the men involved have a healthy regard for the local church (and, further, many will be vigorous denominationalists in their own right), there is not always clarity about the nature of these organisations. For example, what is The Gospel Coalition? What is Affinity, and what is it for? Is either a church body? Is either an association of churches? Is either a denomination? If they claim to be none of these things, but merely a network or coalition or fellowship, do they become *de facto* associations or denominations through arrogating to themselves and operating with many of the same assumptions and functions? What does all this mean for local church identity and practice in, for example, the Gospel Partnerships, where churches are expected to cooperate in the planting of churches that, one must assume, do not answer to the definition of a church for all those involved? If TGC or its equivalents endorse a man (or fail to criticise a departure from true faith or practice) then such an endorsement (or lack of a response to error) often has an effect far beyond the network itself because of the weight of its explicit and implicit endorsements or criticisms.

It must also be noted that many of these groupings are, by their own determination and admission, centre-bounded sets rather than boundary-bounded sets (work with me—it's not my language![8]). That is, they are intended to be attractional, binding people around a common core rather than enclosing people within boundaries which might be disputed.[9] So far, so apparently nice. However, the trouble with that, and with measuring distance to and from the core, is that (despite your best intentions and sincerest hopes) there will be times at which it is necessary to say that— however much you might seem to hold in common with someone—they have stated something that puts them beyond the pale of orthodoxy. As we shall see when we deal with the topic of ecumenism, this has led to some self-inflicted hamstringing, where men who ought to have been censured were not because those who should have exposed their sinful failures at key points were unwilling or unable to do so, having bound themselves to a deliberately boundary-less set. This has produced some unhealthy results.

Consolidation

Fourthly and finally, it is a movement of *consolidation*. Since its beginning, I think it is discernibly evident that this river is broadening and slowing down. Several of its figureheads have been very and vocally opposed to the notion of things slowing down. They say, in effect, the following: 'Things begin as missions, become movements, then turn into museums and finally ossify into monuments ... and we are on mission!' And yet it is already a movement, and such a change is of the nature of things; in part it is the process of maturation. The whole machine is slowing down. There is not the same buzz, the same energy, the same drive as once there was. The river is broader and it is slower. The enthusiasm has shifted slightly and the issues and arguments have developed. I am not saying that there is any less vigour in some quarters, but this is not the rushing mountain stream it once was, with the dynamism simply to carry light things before it. One of the issues coming up more regularly is the idea of succession. Some of the father figures in the movement have talked openly (that is, on blogs and through other media) about what is going to happen after they have moved on. Some of those same senior men in the US— like John Piper—have begun to work out in principle and in practice a handing over to other, younger men (in Piper's case, pastorally, to Jason Meyer, though it remains to be seen what role and influence Piper will retain, formally or informally, within new Calvinism as a whole or the Desiring God subset particularly). Although there remains a central core, others are taking up the mantle and some of the attention is shifting and the drive dissipating. I cannot be absolute, but there seems to be an easing of the pace and an awareness that we are entering a period of transition with regard to new Calvinism.

While this list of defining features is brief and broad and far from exhaustive, I trust that those familiar with the new Calvinism as a whole or with specific manifestations of it will be able to identify some recognizable points of reference in this overview. Taking all these things about the new Calvinism into account, I want to offer first some commendations and then some cautions and concerns, as someone who has appreciated and learned from them in several ways but who has also seen early and somewhat nebulous elements of concern solidify into something more definite and dangerous.

Chapter 3
Commendations

Christ-oriented and God-honouring

The first thing that I particularly appreciate about many new Calvinists is that *they set out to be Christ-oriented and God-honouring*. There may be questions as to the degree of their success in this, but it is right to acknowledge that it is the sincere intention. One of the springs of this movement has been John Piper's concern that God should be glorified, bound up in his notion of 'Christian hedonism' (of which more later). He has recast the first question and answer of the Shorter Catechism to suggest that, 'Man's chief end is to glorify God by enjoying him forever.' We are repeatedly told by Piper and have it echoed by others that 'God is most glorified in us when we are most satisfied in him.' This is the kind of language that drives much of this movement, seeking that Christ be known and made known to the glory of God. As we have already hinted, what it means to glorify God in Christ is often very much a matter of Jonathan Edwards mediated through John Piper, and this distinctive understanding is a keystone in the movement. What we cannot deny is that this movement is substantially and explicitly galvanized by concern for the supremacy of God in Christ and that the Lord of Glory be magnified in all things. That is a good thing—it might even be properly described as being at the very core of what it means to be a Calvinist (remember Warfield)—and something we should embrace as giving us common ground with any man who holds truly to that conviction and its necessary corollaries.

While we must fine tune some of this later and might have strong feelings about whether or not it is being attained, we should recognize that this is the sincere and stated aim of almost all of those involved, and it is in itself heartily to be commended. Indeed, in many instances among individuals and churches it is a desire and a pursuit in principle and in practice that would readily and heartily bring almost any true believer alongside. I should hope that many others could readily express their hearts and raise their voices in the same Scriptural sentiments and desires:

Oh, the depth of the riches both of the wisdom and knowledge of God! How unsearchable are His judgments and His ways past finding out! For who has known the mind of the LORD? Or who has become His counsellor? Or who has first given to Him and it shall be repaid to him? For of Him and through Him and to Him are all things, to whom be glory forever. Amen. (Romans 11:33–36)

Or again:

And every creature which is in heaven and on the earth and under the earth and such as are in the sea, and all that are in them, I heard saying: 'Blessing and honour and glory and power be to Him who sits on the throne, and to the Lamb, forever and ever!' (Revelation 5:13)

There are men individually and churches corporately whose entire notions of what it means to be genuinely Christian have been healthily revolutionized or revitalized by this emphasis. Many have been set on a more biblical track as a result. There is eloquent testimony to this in such developments as the so-called Calvinist resurgence among Southern Baptists, largely reflecting the committed stand and sterling work of Al Mohler and others of his ilk in environments like

Southern Seminary in Louisville, supported by such movements as Mark Dever's 9Marks.

Grace-soaked

Secondly, it is in many respects *a grace-soaked movement*. God's grace in the gospel of Christ has become and has remained amazing to these brothers and sisters. If you read the books, follow the blogs, and listen to the conversations, you will hear 'gospel-this' and 'gospel-that' and 'gospel-the-other,' perhaps almost to the point of inanity (there has to be another adjective you are allowed to use sometimes!). Nevertheless, the gospel is the great thing and therefore Christ and him crucified is at the heart of things. There is a freshness and enthusiasm that comes with this sense of discovery.

You can listen to a man like Matt Chandler seeking to testify of and press home divine mercies in Christ and hear it in the substance and tone of his words. Or again, you can listen to John Piper talk about Jonathan Edwards' views of God's glory and hear the abiding excitement of a man who has discovered something that he once did not know but which now has gripped his soul, and that gives him a vigour, an excitement, a freshness. This is particularly refreshing among some of the older men, who have not become jaded and cool, losing their sense of joyful wonder at God's mercies toward them. For many others in the movement, they have recently come to begin to begin to understand the beauty and the splendour of God's grace in Jesus Christ, and there is a corresponding enthusiasm: it is not old hat but rather new and delightful, and so this contributes to what is in many ways a vibrantly joyful movement. Such friends are excited about the fact that God has loved them in Christ quite apart from their own deserving and that results in a contagious and attractive enthusiasm. They delight to be loved by God in Christ.

Now, we may contend, and rightly, that such gospel-centred joy is not the sole preserve of new Calvinism, and never was. However, those who have some concerns about new Calvinism must consider whether or not we have dealt (or have been perceived to deal) this delight in God's grace the death of a thousand cuts, qualifying and trimming until we are left with very little to show or to express. Have we been guilty of allowing grace to become familiar or suspect, of so guarding our gospel jewels that we have become very slow to enjoy them?

Missional

Thirdly, it is for most of those involved an avowedly *missional* movement. You may or may not like that buzzword, but it is the one in use. The new Calvinism tends to be passionately and sacrificially missional. There is a desire that the glory of God be known in all the earth and so most of those involved seek to preach the gospel and to make disciples (there is a good and healthy emphasis on discipleship in many circles). They want to plant churches and to train preachers. For example, though you may not appreciate the implications of the name, the Acts 29 movement has deliberately set out to encourage and assist churches to plant other church-planting churches, and there has been a significant measure of success on some levels. Similarly, the 9Marks movement among the Southern Baptists, while lacking some of the spikier edges of Acts 29, has seen many churches either planted or revitalized. This concern, generally speaking, is local, national and international. This is a good model. It is, in many respects, a reflection of New Testament Christianity, and obviously that is to be heartily commended. It is a model that too many churches have lost sight of, both in their prayers and in their practices and pursuits.

New Calvinists are often ready to overlook and overcome boundaries that may cripple other people, sometimes because they have been saved from the spiritual regions that others have effectively begun to consider beyond the pale. So they are reaching the lost; many of them are reaching people that others are not. They are going to places some churches do not and perhaps will not go. They are dealing with people of whom others may be scared. They are having doors opened before them that have never opened to some of us and they are taking these opportunities and going to tell people about the Lord Jesus Christ. I think that this is, in essence, wonderful and I wish that it were—in its best and healthiest form—more characteristic of more churches.

Complementarian

Fourthly, it is substantially a *complementarian* movement. By that I mean it seeks to regard men as men and women as women in their proper places and spheres as God has appointed them. For example, several of the leading lights—notably Wayne Grudem, Ray Ortlund, Jr. and John Piper—had a significant role in or some influence on the publication of the 'Danvers Statement' of 1987 which lies largely behind the Council on biblical Manhood and Womanhood (CBMW) and provides a summary of its core beliefs.

Nevertheless, I want to qualify this slightly in two ways. First of all, in keeping with the movement as a whole, this is a spectrum, and there are manifestations of this complementarianism with which not everyone will agree: there would be differences in emphasis and perspective at certain points. To take a couple of examples, some churches and individuals would vigorously endorse female deacons, while The Gospel Coalition's female bloggers and conference 'speakers'

present, at times, some interesting conundrums given
the spheres and the manner in which they operate.

Second, I find it rather amusing that—given all the
things that the new Calvinism seems determined *not* to
be about—complementarianism in the realm of gender
and male/female relationships and responsibilities is
such a significant issue, so much so that I could almost
put this in the list of defining qualities. The new
Calvinists generally make a big deal about the fact that
they are or intend to be biblically complementarian.
That concern works itself out as a corresponding
influence on what it is to have a healthy family life,
what it means to have male leadership in the church,
and other such areas. At times the masculinity (and,
by contrast, the femininity) that is presented becomes
almost a caricature (drifting among men in some circles
toward a sort of hairy, Neanderthal, chest-beating
machismo) but generally they want men to be men and
women to be women. They want that to be so in single
life, in married life, in church life, in family life. This
is a good and appropriate emphasis proving attractive
both to men and women. As women becoming real,
godly women find men who are becoming real, godly
men, and as men are given opportunity to really be men
(especially younger men who are finding models of
masculine headship, of vigour, or passion, of endeavour
in this movement) there is a growing sense of deep

answering unto deep. It is probably one of the reasons why this is a movement of so many younger preachers. One recalls the answer that Lloyd-Jones gave when asked why there were so few young men in the pews: 'Because there are so many old women in the pulpits!' At present, that tends not to be a new Calvinist problem. They have gathered a spearhead of active, energetic and committed (and often stable) young men to preach the gospel in the church and to carry the gospel into the world, alongside of whom are many vigorous, active, energetic, and committed women. I think that is, in essence, a good thing.

Unfortunately, it must also be pointed out that the errant machismo evident in some circles has sometimes slipped even further into a puerile approach to and even an unhealthy focus on sex and sexuality. Indeed, in some circles there seems to be an obsession with sex and sexuality—often excused on the basis of the hypersexuality of the Western culture—which is, at best, out of kilter with the biblical treatment of the topic, and, at worst, a gross example of darkness masquerading as light. Some treatments of sexual sin have put almost as many tempting ideas in the heads of men and women struggling with lust as anything they have come across in the world. There is an insensitivity and a prurience that is unbecoming. Examples would include Mark and Grace Driscoll's recent book *Real Marriage*, with its grid of sexual acts graphically described and assessed on the basis of their legitimacy within marriage,[10] or the cheerful recommendation by the Acts 29 Western Europe website of counsel from a prominent Australian FIEC pastor (in order to 'get a feel for the man and his ministry') who, upon being asked for the advice he would give to young church planters, immediately replied, 'Sex … lots of it … with your wife.'[11] Is that a joke? A good one? Is it serious advice? Really? Did he have time to think that up or was it off the cuff? Which possibility makes it a better answer? How much did his wife appreciate that response? An appropriate and Scriptural straightforwardness with regard to human sexuality is not to be complained at, but the answer to prudishness is not prurience (or vice versa), and where this focus on sex and sexuality loses all sense of perspective and boundaries it becomes something profoundly ugly.

Immersed and inventive

Furthermore, the new Calvinists tend to be both *immersed and inventive*. They are immersed in many things, but I want positively to highlight theology and technology. They are immersed in theology—they are readers. If you engage with some of the book publishing houses, including a good number of the more conservative ones, you will find that their major sales are often in new Calvinistic circles. Crossway is probably the new Calvinist publishing house of choice, and it has been pumping out a steady stream of engaging, well-produced and often outstanding volumes over recent years, as well as being behind the new Calvinist Bible translation of choice, the English Standard Version. Witness, too, the appetite of significant publishers to be giving away books—many of which are actually read, believe it or not—at some of the big conferences. Many new Calvinists are lapping up high grade theological material. They are reading good books and weighty books, as well as engaging with shorter and more ephemeral productions. They love to know more about God. They are often careful and profound thinkers. They want to know how God's truth relates to and works out in the church and the world.

They are inventive and immersed with regard to technology. Of course, much of this will now take place online or feed into that realm. Many are what are called 'early adopters'. The latest smart phone or video technology comes out and they are the first in line; some new platform is developed and new Calvinists are among the first to embrace and employ it. And Apple—it's got to be Apple (at least until something else is cool). If you own a PC you are almost by definition not a new Calvinist. They blog exuberantly and exhaustively (though sometimes forgetting that a few big names and a lot of cross-traffic is not the same as being the dominant voice of Christianity in the electronic ether). They seek to be at the cutting edge of technology in many respects. They are not afraid to use social media and to harness the power of online interaction. Again, you may have questions about the nature and impact of those media, and about the effect of the medium on the very message that it carries. In this respect, it is interesting that Tim Challies—probably *the* cyberspatial gateway for many to all things young, restless and reformed—produced a typically sane and careful consideration of some of these technological issues in a book called *The Next Story* (Zondervan, 2011). However, this book was dismissed in some quarters within the movement for being too reserved and cagey about the use of technology in its many forms, not least the development of the internet. That said, such critics— often seeking to take account of those concerns—say, 'It's here, let's get it, let's use it in order to bring Christ and the gospel to bear on the people who are in these environments.' So they will use both old and new media very effectively to propagate the truth and the new Calvinist take on it.

I put those two elements of theology and technology together because it is very much the movement that carries along the gospel as they themselves teach it. It is not quite one and the same thing, but they do not come separate from each other: the gospel comes dressed in new Calvinist colours and defined by new Calvinist convictions. All this makes them highly visible and very persuasive in the demographic group who are immersed in online culture, and that is almost everyone who is in their thirties and younger. When I first went to university not that long ago, students were encouraged to use computers to submit at least some of their essays; I wonder if anyone now uses a pen to write an essay. It is only in the last ten to twenty years that so much human social interaction has moved online. So anyone in their mid-thirties and younger is almost by definition immersed in that electronic expression of our world unless they have deliberately decided to step away from it. And this is a world that the new Calvinist substantially inhabits, and it is this familiarity which makes them very potent in that narrow sphere.

However, this raises other issues: What if you are not part of that significant online presence? What if you do not live online? What if you know nothing about what a friend of mine calls 'TwitFace'? What if you are part of a generation that either never embraced the internet or which already considers platforms and applications in which the new Calvinism has taken root *passé*? This concentration can lock out some who are not immersed in the same media, but—whether Twitter or Facebook or Snapchat or Instagram or Tumblr or Pinterest or whatever else it may be or may become—some new Calvinists will be among the men and women who will be there first and they will be looking to take advantage of these things to the glory of God.

Preaching

A sixth and final commendation is that this is a movement that, at its best, is *committed in principle to expository preaching*. Again, there are styles and approaches to which I might and would take exception, and there are other things which adhere around the preaching which I would question, but there is among many an underlying commitment to explain and apply the Bible as the Word of God. Many of the leading lights of the movement are pastors and preachers, committed either to systematic expository preaching series or to some other form of expository ministry. The conferences have been, by and large, preaching conferences. Discussions often revolve around what the Bible says and what it means. Books are written expounding the Word of God. There are and there will continue to be discussions about whether or not the expositions, conclusions and applications are accurate— the same sort of often-healthy discussions as happen within, across and between other circles. Nevertheless, this commitment at least provides some common ground for the discussion to advance: 'What does the

Bible say?' Where this principle is espoused and not undermined, a common foundation allows for a mutual pursuit of the truth as it is in Jesus.

Summary

These are not the only commendations, but they are at least six areas where I have appreciated and learned from some of the emphases of true brothers and sisters within new Calvinist circles. I can sincerely say that I would be glad to be carefully described in these fundamentally positive terms, and I am glad to recognise these excellent things, and I hope that many others would be also.

For some, such a list will not go far enough. Others may feel that any commendations are out of place. However, please consider again the spectrum with which we are dealing. You will take into account that not all of these commendations belong to all of those who call themselves new Calvinists, at least not to the same degree, but they do belong to some, even many. It would be unrighteous to neglect or despise those good things which are present, even if some must be qualified. This is true for at least three reasons.

First, I think we ought to learn from Barnabas at this point. Consider what happened after the death of Stephen:

Now those who were scattered after the persecution
that arose over Stephen travelled as far as Phoenicia,
Cyprus, and Antioch, preaching the word to no one but
the Jews only. But some of them were men from Cyprus
and Cyrene, who, when they had come to Antioch, spoke
to the Hellenists, preaching the Lord Jesus. And the hand
of the Lord was with them, and a great number believed
and turned to the Lord. Then news of these things came
to the ears of the church in Jerusalem, and they sent out
Barnabas to go as far as Antioch. When he came and had
seen the grace of God, he was glad, and encouraged them
all that with purpose of heart they should continue with
the Lord. For he was a good man, full of the Holy Spirit
and of faith. And a great many people were added to the
Lord. Then Barnabas departed for Tarsus to seek Saul.
And when he had found him, he brought him to Antioch.
So it was that for a whole year they assembled with the
church and taught a great many people. And the disciples
were first called Christians in Antioch. (Acts 11:19–26)

I do not intend to draw parallels that do not exist,
but I do suggest that we would do well to recognise
the grace of God and to be glad when we see it, and to
encourage those who enjoy it 'that with purpose of heart
they should continue with the Lord' (Acts 11:23). While
that should not blind us to problems and weaknesses, I
would suggest that it is a healthy spirit, finding much of

its form and expression in 1 Corinthians 13, and worthy of emulation. Besides, who knows how many Sauls or Apolloses (Acts 18:24–26) there are to be drawn in and trained up for the work of the kingdom?

Second, if God chooses to draw a straight line with a crooked stick (and when, using sinful men—including us—as his means, is this ever not the case?) then should I not rejoice at the straightness of the line even if I acknowledge a degree of crookedness in the stick? Given the cautions and concerns to come, we might legitimately consider that the new Calvinism represents a backward step for some. However, what of the man or woman who has known nothing of the true God before meeting him savingly through this movement, or who has been walking in theological gloom until obtaining a measure of light through these teachers? Surely such blessings ought never to be despised! If a sinner is pointed to Christ, saved from sin, death and hell, and put into the path of Christian pilgrimage or advanced along it through the ministry of any man, I can legitimately rejoice, even while wishing that the way might be more clearly defined. If a man who starts with nothing comes by this route to obtain something of eternal value, I can and will praise the God of salvation.

Third, I am happy to be found in the company of Matthew Henry, who commented in this way on Luke 7:10.

Note, Christ will have those that follow him to observe and take notice of the great examples of faith that are sometimes set before them—especially when any such are found among those that do not follow Christ so closely as they do in profession—that we may be shamed by the strength of their faith out of the weakness and waverings of ours.

If I am persuaded that some do not follow Christ in practice so closely as they do in profession, it does not mean that I cannot learn from the strength of their faith.

Let me conclude this section by suggesting that, *at its best*, the new Calvinism is a God-centred movement. Insofar as this is so, we should both recognise it and rejoice because of it. It is easy to adopt a vinegary attitude that is determined to see no good in anyone with any remote association with anyone who once shook hands with a new Calvinist but which fails to take account of the spectrum along which this movement lies. Where there are no aberrations which genuinely compromise these commendations (and there are many instances in which our assessment can and should be substantially positive) and where there exists significant overlap, or where there are common causes in which we can, without conceding anything weighty, properly cooperate, I believe and hope that with mutual affection and respect we can stand together on matters of first importance and shared interest.

Chapter 4
Cautions and concerns

I also have some cautions and concerns about the new Calvinism. While enjoying some of the emphases and appreciating some of the engagement that these men and women have with the world at large, is there anything here of which to take a more careful and less positive account? As I seek to understand and appreciate the new Calvinism, I have asked myself whether or not there is anything that I might wish to strain out, anything which particularly needs to be tempered, anything—indeed—which needs to be vigorously resisted? Again, consider that we are dealing with a spectrum. Some of the men commended above are also subject to this critique, some more so and some less. Some within the movement would offer very much the same critiques about other ships from the shipyard, and even some of those sailing under the same flag. While we will try to take this into account in our conclusions, let me suggest some cautions and concerns that may ring true.

Pragmatism and commercialism

First of all, there is in many new Calvinists *a tendency to pragmatism and commercialism*. I usually enjoy the American entrepreneurial spirit, the 'Go west, young man!' mentality that I still see in American culture but which is often lacking in Europe (having said that, west of Europe is the Atlantic, so there may be some legitimacy to our scepticism at this point). However, I believe that in some parts of the new Calvinism the entrepreneurial spirit has run amok. This can take various forms of varying degree: for example, Redeemer Presbyterian Church in Manhattan, where Tim Keller pastors, has decided—for the sake of the kind of excellence that it is believed will attract and impress cultured unbelievers—to employ professional but unconverted musicians to assist in their worship services. More abruptly, Mark Driscoll writes that 'a church must determine what size they would like to become and start acting like a church of that size if they hope to achieve that goal … each church must ask how large they want to be and prepare to work toward that goal.'[12]

In such ways, more or less, a principle of pragmatism is applied where it was never meant to be applied. I see a more commercial attitude toward 'doing church.' Listen to that phrase: how do you *do* church? The idea is to get big, then stay big and get bigger. You need to market yourself well and make sure you have got the right people in place. So, at its most crass, if a certain individual—a deacon, for example—is getting in the way of progress, you remove that individual and replace him with someone who can actually do the job that the other is not prepared or not able to do. That is almost a commercial hire-and-fire model, and does not take account of a man's fitness for office or his recognition by the whole church. You need to expand the business? You get rid of the wrong people and find the right people, bringing in workers with the right skill sets to move things forward in accordance with your church (business) model. At points it seems to be a principial lack of principle, as if where the Bible does not overtly address a matter we are free to do whatever we please. I am not suggesting that I have heard that said, but if you step back and consider various operations it does seems as if that is how it actually works in practice. We might imagine that a 'normative principle of life' (or, at least, 'of ecclesiology') is being applied, as if to say, 'If God hasn't explicitly said this isn't a good idea, let's try it!' Here is the flip side of that desire to engage and get the gospel out. The question becomes not, 'What is right?' but 'What will work?' It appears that if something seems to work (*i.e.* if it contributes to bigness, makes an impact) it must be good because it is advancing the mission. Church growth becomes a function of mechanics, of effective systems and programmes. Someone might respond by querying whether there are biblical principles to apply, but—'No! We have to get the word out and we'll use whatever means we can to accomplish that.' This can lead to a pursuit of bigness, of numbers, of profile, for their own sake. When *Time* magazine proclaimed the new Calvinism as one of the 'ten ideas changing the world right now,'[13] immediately this sector of the blogosphere was awash with self-congratulation: 'Wow! We're important, they're listening to us, we've got a seat at culture's table!' Really? Is that what it is all about? Is that what we are pursuing? What happens when the world does not recognize us? Will the gospel have lost its power, or will we need to change things once more to win back the world's commendations? Does God not delight to turn these things on their heads? '"Not by might nor by power, but by My Spirit," says the LORD of Hosts' (Zechariah 4:6).

Some readers may be aware of recent difficulties experienced by Sovereign Grace Ministries, having to do with certain claims of abuse dating back several decades. My point here relates not to the nature of the problem, but to the fact that these tensions were of sufficient magnitude to receive national press attention in the United States. However, in covering the story, the Associated Press report's first line described this group as 'a small evangelical Christian denomination called Sovereign Grace Ministries.'[14] Please do not misunderstand this reference as gloating about either the problems or the description. I offer it merely as a demonstration—a perceptual corrective, if you will—of how small some big fish are actually thought to be by the wider world (even the wider Christian world), even when they are recognised in it. This may in itself offer some comfort to those who are small, and smaller yet, in remembering how the Lord loves to work with the lowly and despised.

Alongside and because of this we are faced with reams of statistics—new Calvinists often love statistics! There is nothing inherently wrong with statistics—more than 75% of people will tell you that—but it depends on how they are wielded. Listen to some of the sermons: the introduction begins, 'Statistics say that this is important, so this is a good and relevant topic to deal with this morning.' Mark Driscoll is a purveyor *par excellence* of this approach: watch a few videos and you will be able to parrot that Seattle is (was?) one of the least-churched cities in America, has (had?) more dogs than Christians, and so on and so forth. A survey says this, and churches are like that, and so we need to adapt and respond to what this latest survey says about the state of the church and the state of the world.

Furthermore, there is an ugly showmanship about some of it. There is more than a hint of performance, often something overly dramatic or slickly cultured in some of the preaching and presentation. Indeed, in some circles, there is explicit encouragement to study the methods and mannerisms of worldly entertainers and to employ them for the kingdom, forgetting that 'the weapons of our warfare are not carnal but mighty in God for pulling down strongholds, casting down arguments and every high thing that exalts itself against the knowledge of God, bringing every thought into captivity to the obedience of Christ' (2 Cor. 10:4–5). There are gimmicks that creep in, with the associated concern that if you have attracted people by means of performances and gimmicks, you will need ever more extravagant performances or ever more extreme gimmicks in order to keep their attention. There are times in which men in and around this movement run the church more like a commercial enterprise than they minister to it as the body of Christ.

All this leads to an emphasis on and appreciation of size that can become profoundly unhealthy. The virtue of bigness is promoted for its own sake, and it can sometimes appear that a man with a significant profile and a vast number of followers can rise above criticism. Weight of numbers—people, downloads, services, churches, books—counts, and the headcount becomes a virtue in its own right. Perhaps this is what is driving, in part, the worrying trend toward what are called multi-campus churches. This scheme usually involves larger churches that are organised around the ministry of one prominent figure. Enabled by the technology now available, they establish a variety of venues in which satellite congregations gather to hear, either live or with some kind of time-lag (occasionally allowing a sort of edited highlights package to be compiled!), the teaching of the main man. Although we are often assured that each of the campus congregations has its own eldership, the fact remains that the whole revolves around the core figure, who has—to all intents and purposes—become the indispensable hub of the whole operation, sitting at the centre of some kind of ecclesiastical franchise. Without wishing to divert into a different discussion, such practices raise a host of questions about the nature of the church, the role of pastors and preachers, the care of the flock, the operations of the Holy Spirit in preaching, but the draw of the celebrity preacher and his ability to gather not only a crowd but a number of crowds, seems to trump any more substantial considerations. In a series of sermons preached in 1969, Dr Martyn Lloyd-Jones made the prescient comment that 'we are rapidly getting to the stage in which there will be only two or three preachers—if even that many—in the world. And the rest of the world will be listening to them on tapes or on television or something else.'[15] Although his concern arose in a different context, where the pursuit of bigness and numbers dominates, church-planting and building can too quickly become an exercise in legal entities recognized, targets achieved, and profiles raised rather than lost souls saved and real congregations established. Such a spirit has allowed men who have garnered substantial followings to operate with little or no challenge from others, often hiding behind the defence that something which works (the numbers being the evidence) must be worthy, must be right, must be evidence of God's blessing. We see this, for example, in the willingness of some to engage with T. D. Jakes (see below), or the apparent softening toward someone of numerical supremacy like Joel Osteen hinted at by Mark Driscoll in an interview on a recent book. Driscoll said:

> I am aware of the theological differences that exist between our tribe and Pastor Joel. I also know my Reformed brothers like to treat Pastor Joel like a piñata, but there are worse things than being happy and encouraging at a time when the most common prescription medications are antidepressants. A few guys

in our tribe could learn to talk about something other than painful, arduous suffering once and a while—if nothing else than for the sake of variety. Our identity is not in our joy, and our identity is not in our suffering. Our identity is in Christ, whether we have joy or are suffering.[16]

Here again is the tribal language, and here, perhaps, is the readiness to learn from someone who is bigger because if they are bigger, then by definition they have something to teach us. Such an emphasis does not serve the church of God well, any more than does the proclamation of smallness and ineffectiveness as an inherent mark of faithfulness and purity. (As Carl Trueman has pointed out, 'not revelling in smallness and irrelevance does not require that I necessarily regard increasing numerical and financial size as accurate gauges of fidelity and truth.'[17]) I wonder how much of this is driving the pursuit of conglomeration? Certainly one of the arguments often used in the UK for the support of certain groupings is that as long as there are enough of us, the world will have to listen to us. This claim is, of course, patent nonsense in the spiritual realm (though it may have some limited substance in the social-political-cultural sphere), but it has enough appearance of credibility to be persuasive to many. Without equating smallness with purity or

insignificance with faithfulness, we must remember
God's pattern of working and his people's enduring
expectation: 'Now I know that the LORD saves His
anointed; He will answer him from His holy heaven
with the saving strength of His right hand. Some trust in
chariots, and some in horses; but we will remember the
name of the LORD our God' (Psalm 20:6–7).

Culture

A second concern lies in *an unbalanced view of culture*.
A neo-Kuyperian perspective dominates the movement.
Perhaps the keynote is this statement from Kuyper:
'There is not a square inch in the whole domain of
human existence over which Christ, who is sovereign
over all, does not shout, "Mine!"'[18] That translates, in
some parts of the new Calvinist spectrum, as a sense that
this world is neutral territory. We are in no man's land
and therefore culture is all up for grabs: no distinction
is permitted between the sacred and the secular, or
even the profane—for some, such distinctions are
part of evangelicalism's anti-intellectualism.[19] We are
conquering culture for King Jesus, therefore nothing
is out of bounds. We can take anything this world
produces and we can Christianize it. Paul's statement
that 'I have become all things to all men, that I might
by all means save some' (1 Corinthians 9:22) is taken
out of context and becomes a corporate slogan opening

the door to all manner of activity rather than the legitimate accommodation of the individual believer to the consciences of those around him, often a matter of sacrificing personal liberties rather than demanding them.

One of the classic examples would be something like musical forms. We are encouraged to embrace all musical forms (though, for some reason, it is rap and hip-hop which seem to be the hills on which everyone has chosen to die) and the uniforms and behaviours that go with them. We can apparently take the structures that communicate those particular things and embrace them as Christians. We can do this because the forms and the uniforms and the structures and the behaviours are all neutral, or so generationally conditioned as to be without enduring substance or biblical principle,[20] and we just need to make them carry a Christian message. I am not saying that there is no cultural element to or component of worship in any church or environment, but my concern is with the underlying principles rather than with the outworked practice.

This attitude to culture can become an over-realized hope, almost an over-realized eschatology, a confusion between what is 'not yet' and what is 'already' in the life of the kingdom. Such thinking has gone beyond the Scriptural norm. Some new Calvinists can be so concerned to be relevant and accessible that they become slaves to hipness. Read some of their books and everything is defined by a narrow target audience. Not so long ago you had to reference *The Matrix* (although frankly that is already a little old school) and then it was *The Lord of the Rings* (and that will be out-of-date before long, but at least we have *The Hobbit* to keep us going for a while). Then you go for the higher end of the cultural spectrum, where things might be a little more enduring, and make reference to Flannery O'Connor and then you might pander to the intellectuals by talking about C. S. Lewis. You get a mass of cultural buzzwords, riding the wave of the latest big film series or the book that everyone is or should be talking about.

There is a sense in which some are doing something well here. They are looking into the sphere in which they are operating. They are trying to understand the language and the culture with which they are dealing and they are sincerely trying to bring the gospel to bear, but it often feels like a checklist to prove how cutting-edge they are: 'I've read all the latest books and I've seen all the latest films.' [21] It is an almost-obsession that becomes very easy to mock and mimic. The underlying assumption is that culture is neutral and therefore up for grabs; we just need to use it as the vehicle to bring Christ to bear.

There are two particular areas in which you will see this working itself out: one is worship and the other is evangelism. Again, generally speaking, the new Calvinism does not embrace the regulative principle of worship. I recognise that this is a generalisation, and—again—we must recognise a spectrum. However, I believe that any extended exposure to most of the churches or the variety of conferences which would be happy counting themselves as aligned with the new Calvinists would demonstrate the validity of this assertion. Accommodation in the matter of church worship is, among some, almost a given in the light of the evangelistic methodology embraced. Even in a more sober stream like 9Marks, and taking a more thoughtful and balanced approach, there seems to be a measure of confusion. Amidst much that is helpful in their material,[22] we can isolate a statement like the following: 'The regulative principle says that Scripture regulates what is permissible to do in public worship. And those who hold the regulative principle will approach each question carefully, asking not merely "What will God allow?" but also "What does God prefer?"'[23] Historically, however, the regulative principle asks neither, 'What will God allow?' or 'What does God prefer?' but 'What does God require?'.

Moving further, it seems to me that the vast majority of new Calvinists believe that all of life is worship (a phrase you will hear time and time again, often without a great deal of nuance[24]). There is a sense in which that is true: 'whether you eat or drink, or whatever you do, do all to the glory of God' (1 Corinthians 10:31) and 'whatever you do in word or deed, do all in the name of the Lord Jesus, giving thanks to God the Father through Him' (Colossians 3:17) would both bear that out in measure. Who would deny that all of life must be lived before the eye of God? But what happens if everything becomes worship in precisely the same way? What happens if everything is flattened out? Then there are no peaks or troughs in our experience of coming before God to bring glory and honour to him. There are no high points and rather than *everything* being worship, *nothing* is worship. It is this very reversal that often leads to an aping of the world. A deliberate process takes place in which our worship will be as much like the activity of the world as possible (after all, all of life is worship) but we will just Christianize it. So if our target audience is basically indie kids,[25] we'll get an indie-style Christian band to sing Christian lyrics in indie style (or indie lyrics with a Christian flavour—either way will work) and then we will preach the gospel. To pick up on an earlier point, there is also a danger that the embrace of current forms carries with it certain current emphases: some though not all of the more modern hymnody will reflect the shallow and angst-ridden self-centredness of the modern West.

This process of contextualization—cultural adaptation

or accommodation—is embraced at various different points in various different spheres and with varying degrees of legitimacy. So with regard to worship, if we accept that we are always worshipping God and all of culture is up for grabs, there is no needed distinction between the sacred and the profane. That also bleeds over into evangelism because the issue becomes a matter of finding that which attracts people, whatever seems to work. As long as they are coming to hear and as long as we have claimed this thing—whatever 'this thing' may be—for Jesus then it no longer matters what forms it takes. I am not suggesting that no people are being reached and none of them are being saved, but the underlying pragmatism together with this view of culture have a tendency to make evangelism drift toward becoming more like the world in order to win the world. Some have suggested that this is really a Calvinistic soteriology allied to an Arminian methodology, and there is more than a grain of truth in the assertion. The motives may be good and the ends commendable in themselves, but the means are wrong.

It is also worth noting that this appetite for cultural and often academic engagement (which often becomes a desire or need for acceptance with if not quite applause from the world) may be eroding other doctrinal distinctives of historic Reformed Christianity.

For example, Tim Keller, a prominent man in this

movement, has spoken without biblical clarity and robustness at certain key points. On the nature of sin and on atonement, Keller can say that 'God did not, then, inflict pain on someone else, but rather on the Cross absorbed the pain, violence and evil of the world into himself … this is a God who becomes human and offers his own lifeblood in order to honor moral justice and merciful love so that someday he can destroy all evil without destroying us.'[26] The cutting edge of penal substitutionary atonement seems, at best, muted at this point, reduced from the imposition of wrath and curse to the absorption of pain and violence. An organisation called BioLogos—dedicated to promoting theistic evolution, and describing itself as 'a community of evangelical Christians committed to exploring and celebrating the compatibility of evolutionary creation and biblical faith'[27]—boasts a commendation from Keller, as follows:

Many people today, both secular and Christian, want us to believe that science and religion cannot live together. Not only is this untrue, but we believe that a thoughtful dialogue between science and faith is essential for engaging the hearts and minds of individuals today. The BioLogos Foundation provides an important first step towards that end.[28]

Keller's typically measured language might not seem to be a ringing endorsement, but he continues to participate in BioLogos, and has prepared a vague 'white paper' for the organisation,[29] the inconclusive conclusion of which suggests

> that Christians who are seeking to correlate Scripture and science must be a 'bigger tent' than either the anti-scientific religionists or the anti-religious scientists. Even though in this paper I argue for the importance of belief in a literal Adam and Eve, I have shown here that there are several ways to hold that and still believe in God using E[voluntionary] B[iolgoical] P[rocesses].[30]

I am not seeking to single Keller out unfairly, but I fear that the pressure for acceptability that often goes with this approach to culture, the two-way street that can develop without any thought of setting up appropriate roadblocks, may well lead to further watering down of doctrine in critical areas, especially among those who will follow in the footsteps of these leaders.[31]

Holiness

The third caution or concern is that many within new Calvinism manifest *a troubling approach to holiness*. There are two elements here. The first is what I consider to be incipient antinomianism. Antinomianism in this context refers, in essence, to those who do not believe in the abiding validity of the moral law for those who are in Christ Jesus. I call it incipient because it is there in seed form even if it is not yet fully broken out in doctrine or in practice. As so often, the fourth commandment—the matter of the new covenant Sabbath, the Lord's day—is usually the first point of contact.[32] Many of the leading lights in the new Calvinist movement would formally embrace or at least align themselves toward what is sometimes called New Covenant Theology.[33] Indeed, D. A. Carson's volume *From Sabbath to Lord's Day* (Wipf & Stock, 1999), and more specifically his treatment of Matthew 5:17–18, has been a seminal text for the movement away from sabbatarianism, even if we are told that Carson's personal practice is almost identical to those who hold to a Lord's day rest as part of the new covenant.

This is where we come back to the fact that some of these are holy men who seem to be able to hold some curious things, even contradictory things, in tension and yet continue to pursue godliness. (I am not singling out D. A. Carson in the material that follows, nor accusing him of these specifics.) They are not always saying that there is absolutely no law; sometimes it works out more as a neonomianism (like that of Richard Baxter) in which Christ in effect resets the scales and we walk according to a new and more readily attainable standard. Others will discuss, with some nuance, what is sometimes described as a republication or reiteration of the moral law, or elements of it, in the New Testament, considered to be 'the law of Christ'. But it is becoming a casual and ill-considered mantra, repeated in endless blog discussions and trolled out in countless videos and articles, that we are no longer under law but that we are under grace. For many, what this means—and this is the corollary that is argued over—is that we follow Christ but that is not related to embracing and obeying the Ten Commandments. I suspect that a straw poll of British evangelicalism would suggest that a casual disregard for the Ten Commandments as perpetually binding, based on the woolly sense that the law is bad, and we are under grace, is fairly typical. It was not so long ago that a prominent Baptist like John Ryland Jr. could write of his mentor, Robert Hall Sr., concerning 'the denial of the law of God as a rule of conduct to believers' that 'he ever considered [this sentiment] as so gross a piece of *Antinomianism*, that he did not suppose any man could embrace it, whose conscience was not seared as with a hot iron.'[34] I am not suggesting that practical antinomianism is rife, but the basis and standard of our obedience is shifting, and—as it does so—we are seeing and, I fear, will see an increasing number of Christians falling into gross sin, perhaps without any sense of its sinfulness.

The second element is related to this. An ongoing discussion continues about the nature of sanctification. Two men who have engaged in this, and who help to showcase the issue, are Tullian Tchividjian of Cape Coral, Florida, and Kevin DeYoung in Lansing, Michigan. Kevin DeYoung is pushing for the more orthodox perspective, and doing so very helpfully,[35] whereas Tchividjian is concerned that there is not enough grace in that process and suggesting more that we are sanctified by faith.[36] You might well ask, 'But can you be sanctified without faith? Can you become more like Jesus Christ without faith?' Of course you cannot, and this should never be denied. This is a process in which we continue to rely upon the grace of God in Christ. It is in union with Jesus Christ in his death to sin and resurrection life that his power works in us. It is on account of our relationship to Christ that the Holy Spirit takes up residence in our hearts, and we are then conformed to the image of God's Son. This is a gracious relationship grounded in faith. So there is certainly a need for faith if we are to be sanctified, and we depend upon the grace of God every moment in our sanctification. Nevertheless, we are not sanctified by faith (as a sort of pre-emptive beatific vision) in the same way that we are justified by faith. A false dichotomy is being established between faith and duty or effort and I think that some of this goes back to Piper's idea that we glorify God by enjoying him forever, that God is most glorified in me when I am most satisfied in him. (Please note that John Piper speaks very definitely of the need to pursue and attain genuine holiness as a part of our being saved, although he seems to resist any language of duty or gratitude in our response to grace.[37]) Indeed, I have begun to see it argued that it is not possible that God should be glorified unless I am also being immediately satisfied, that if I am not being satisfied then God cannot be glorified. The focus has ended up on self-satisfaction rather than God-glorification. This has become, for some, a test of action, and it is not one that makes the glory of God the chief end of man, but swings the focus to where it does not belong—on the desires and appetites of the creature.

But why be afraid of the words duty and obedience and commandment? Some in this movement are so concerned to talk about grace that it is almost as if an overreaction has occurred against some of these notions of effort and obedience and duty, which are part of what we do as those who enjoy the grace of God in Jesus Christ. The language of Philippians 2:12–13—'Therefore, my beloved, as you have always obeyed, not as in my presence only, but now much more in my absence, work out your own salvation with fear and trembling; for it is God who works in you both to will and to do for His good pleasure'—seems to be almost anathema to some, needing to be explained away or worked around.

A concern not to be or become legalists has driven some back toward antinomianism. I appreciate the concern, and the possibility that some are reacting against an unnecessary and unscriptural rigidity, but one wearies of hearing, in essence, the same mantra: 'I used to be a legalist, but I got better.' We are, it seems, all recovering Pharisees. I rarely hear of anyone boasting that they are a recovering tax collector. On the one hand, much of this criticism defines legalism wrongly (accurately, legalism is the assumption that a man can get right and/or stay right with God by means of his own efforts), or seems to presume that the antidote to legalism is a smidgen of antinomianism, which would fall close to the category of frying pans and fires.

But the Christian is liberated in order to be holy! Principled obedience is not legalism. What is the pattern and framework of my holiness? It is God as he makes himself known in Jesus Christ, Christ being the perfect transcript of what God is like and the perfect embodiment of God's holiness, a holiness made known in his law, a holiness to which the saints are called, in the pursuit of which they are exhorted to labour, and to the attainment of which they are assured, being predestined to be conformed to the image of Christ.

It is as if the focus on gospel indicatives[38] has blinded

some to their connection with gospel imperatives[39] (remembering that any concern you might have about this should not lead you to become wary of the indicatives and make our sole preserve the imperatives). To preach the imperatives without the indicatives is to impose burdens and give no strength to carry them, and this would be an equally false emphasis. Indicative and imperatives are yoked together. We are redeemed for holiness. Because God is at work in us both to will and to do for his good pleasure, therefore we are to work out our own salvation with fear and trembling. The will of God is our sanctification, and we are commanded to be holy even as he is holy. Here we must preserve the distinction between justification and sanctification. Our works play no part in our justification: in that matter, God the righteous Judge requires an absolute obedience which no sinful man can provide, for the sinner needs a full atonement for sin and the provision of a righteousness that is fully acceptable to God, all of which is provided in Christ alone. But as a justified man, the Lord God becomes my Father, and I strive to please him and delight to know that I can do so in dependence upon Christ and his Spirit. This is not to smuggle works back into a relationship of grace, but rather to give sanctification its full and Scriptural weight and form, without for one moment undermining the blessings and beauties of our justification. We are called to Christ in order that we might be holy, and we must hold fast to the whole of that. Both the indicatives and the imperatives of the gospel must be given their full force in their proper connection. Where this proportion and relationship is not maintained a new legalism—bizarrely but not unusually—can too readily creep in. For example, I recall hearing one very sincere young woman pray in this way: 'Lord, you are not going to ask us if we came to church, or if we read our Bibles, but you are going to ask us what we have done for you.' If that statement is brought into the realm of justification it is fatal, for it shifts the locus of our standing with God away from one set of Christian duties and on to another, replacing a legal spirit which takes refuge in religious formalism with a legal spirit seeking refuge in religious activism. If it is applied in the realm of sanctification, one might ask on what basis this league table of obedience and, by implication, Christian standing has been instituted and by whom, for it tends to elevate the outward and the apparently radical over the inward and seemingly less spectacular.

To return to the main point, where this incipient antinomianism makes its entrance, tensions take root. We must resist the conflation of justification and sanctification, and clarify the confusion over the process of sanctification (a concern that we do not evacuate grace and faith from the process of sanctification which too often leaves us with a process that is made to consist in faith alone). The patterns of history suggest that—as you work down and out from the men who seem able to hold these things together while simultaneously pursuing biblical holiness—succeeding generations will fail to hold those elements in tension. The result will be an increasing abandonment of genuine, full-orbed, new covenant holiness. I am not suggesting that this is the intention, but I believe that this will be the result.

I recognize that by suggesting that many new Calvinists are in principle antinomians I will be accused of being grossly uncharitable—up goes the cry, 'How dare you call us antinomian!' But the very next accusation is likely to be that I am a legalist, so at least we are all square. Again, let me point out that legalism is the pursuit of obedience with the intention of earning acceptance or merit and *not* the pursuit of obedience in accordance with God's law as one redeemed by grace. Furthermore, I have seen some insightful comments on this discussion: someone had dared to use the word 'antinomianism' to describe the kind of approach outlined above, and it had immediately sparked the usual accusations of a legal spirit in the man who had used the word. It was at this point that someone else who did not believe in the abiding validity of the moral law stepped in with a sensible and sincere response: 'Why,' he said, 'are we getting so angry about the use of the word "antinomian." If they are right, that is precisely what we are. I do not believe that they are right, and so I would deny the label. But if they are right, then that is the accurate term for what I believe.' This is refreshing honesty!

If then, we are right in our assessment above—and I am persuaded from Scripture and history that we are—then this is a nascent form of antinomianism that is characteristic of much though not all of the new Calvinism. My fear is that this view will become very attractive to people who want the privileges and benefits and eased conscience of a Christian profession without the demand for holiness being pressed into their hearts resulting in the vigorous pursuit of godliness. Clearly this is not the intention of the new Calvinists by and large. They are not saying, 'Let us sin, then, that grace may abound.' But my concern is that this teaching may create an atmosphere in which liberty is made a cloak for license.

Ecumenism

A fourth caution or concern is *a potentially dangerous ecumenism*. There is a pursuit of unity that may end up being at the expense of truth. Remember that this is an eclectic movement, a spectrum not a monolith. There are men all along the spectrum who do not see eye to eye on certain things. The fact that they can be united on things that are of critical and central importance could be and sometimes is a wonderful testimony to Christian unity. It is a good and a healthy thing in itself, and peace among brothers is a genuine blessing and much to be desired and pursued. However, within new Calvinism in the US a distinction is sometimes made between state and national boundaries. So, for example, the national boundary is what makes us all part of the same kingdom: we are all Christians together. State boundaries, by contrast, would be the distinctions between denominations, or with regard to certain practices or convictions. So some of us are more confessional; some of us are more charismatic. Some of us are baptists; some are paedobaptists. These are lower walls between states within a single nation under God, as it were. In the UK, the national/state parallels do not function in the same way, but we see precisely the same discussion taking place under the rubric of primary and secondary truths.

But who gets to decide which are the state boundaries and which are the national boundaries? I would suggest that it is not the sole remit of those who like and are proposing the idea of state and national boundaries. Who defines what truth is primary and what truth is secondary? It is easy to answer, 'God does.' Fair enough, but who communicates that divine designation to me? My perspective or yours on what should or should not be a primary/national and what should or should not be a secondary/state boundary might be different—perhaps radically different—from someone else's perspective. Depending on who is allowed to categorize and to draw the boundaries, the result can be some very strange bedfellows.

Furthermore, such distinction can lead to a doctrinal minimalism in the name of cooperation. One must ask where the emphasis lies: does it lie in the fact that some truth is primary or secondary, or does it lie in the fact that we are handling *truth*? To be sure, we all recognise that there are some things that are more important than others, and we should have no wish to fall under the proper condemnation of our Lord:

> For you pay tithe of mint and anise and cummin, and have neglected the weightier matters of the law: justice and mercy and faith. These you ought to have done, without leaving the others undone. Blind guides, who strain out a gnat and swallow a camel! (Matthew 23:23–24)

At the same time, that principled pursuit of conglomeration mentioned earlier can lead to an erosion not just of distinctiveness but a downplaying of truth in the name of unity.

In giving specific examples of how this has worked out, it is again necessary to identify particular individuals. In the last few years John Piper's national conferences have included—among some who many of us would be more than eager to hear preach and who a few of us might cross oceans simply to hear pray— such speakers as Douglas Wilson and Rick Warren. These men are receiving what is in essence the Piper stamp of approval. Remember that John Piper has been and remains one of the men who is prominent to the point of pre-eminent, one of the figureheads of this movement. I would suggest to you that, however attractive their personalities, evident their natural gifts, and impressive their profiles, such men as Douglas Wilson (in his guise as a prime exponent of the Federal Vision) and Rick Warren (who seems to be a sort of religious chameleon) are moving past—if not already beyond—the pale of historic biblical Christianity, albeit in very different ways. To bring these men in and to give them one of the most visible platforms in this movement is an exceedingly dangerous thing. When challenged over the involvement of Rick Warren, John Piper responded by interviewing Rick Warren and giving him what amounted to a theological rubber stamping.[40] Again, although Piper may be able to say, 'I'll take this but I won't take that,'[41] the result for many will be the sense, 'Well, Doug Wilson must be entirely reliable,' or, 'Rick Warren must be a credible guide.' It easily leads to a suspension of discernment in which one is tempted to take a draught of poison alongside a drop of tonic. While the desire for Christian unity is a good thing in itself, here is that potentially and actually dangerous ecumenism in which some of these men are reaching beyond the bounds of what is safe and orthodox in terms of credible biblical Christianity.

Perhaps the most significant and instructive occasions in this regard have been James MacDonald's 'Elephant Room' events. James MacDonald was a high profile member—after all, he had a big church—of The Gospel Coalition council. MacDonald hosted a series of meetings in which various men considered brothers in Christ were invited to discuss matters on which they would have different opinions. Operating on and beyond the fringes of new Calvinism, MacDonald had as a guest a man named Perry Noble, who discussed— among other things—his publicly avowed aim (on which he followed through) to open his Easter Sunday services one year with the AC/DC paean to their 'promised land,' *Highway to Hell.* His stated intention was 'to p*** off the religious people.'[42] According to his later testimony, he arrived at this decision after much concerted prayer. Others involved on that occasion included men of the calibre of Steven Furtick. All this was, at the time, largely ignored or substantially brushed under the carpet in TGC circles.

However, the furore really kicked off when

MacDonald invited T. D. Jakes—the well-known prosperity gospel preacher and outspoken modalist[43]— to participate in the Elephant Room 2. How, it was asked, could MacDonald consider a heretic to be a brother in Christ? MacDonald responded not with repentance, but by changing the definition of the Elephant Room to allow someone like Jakes to be involved. A further defence seemed to be the bigness and therefore importance and credibility of the ministries these men had fathered. In fairness, at this point principled men like Mark Dever publicly distanced themselves from the debacle, refusing to participate. The discussion itself was chaired by Mark Driscoll, who—much like John Piper in his *apologia* for Rick Warren a couple of years earlier, but with bells and whistles—sent up a few soft balls for Jakes to smash back, avoiding most of the contentious issues and pressing none of the important ones, before Driscoll and MacDonald effectively welcomed the heretic with open arms into the family of Christ, fawning over a man who has built a huge church and following and ignoring the fact that these have been built on a foundation of damnable error.[44] Of at least equal concern with the event itself was the fact that MacDonald and Driscoll went about this, though not with the express imprimatur of The Gospel Coalition, yet nevertheless while members in good standing of its council and without any real public kickback from TGC as a whole. With the defence given that those on the outside could not possibly know all that was taking place on the inside, Don Carson and Tim Keller provided a lengthy, interesting but largely inconclusive overview of issues they believe to be related to this debate.[45] They gave a lot of information, they demonstrated their erudition, they offered their assurance that 'top men' were on the job, but left many spectators more than a little confused about what they were trying to achieve. In keeping with much of the response, this official declaration was a substantially boneless piece, providing no definition, drawing no lines, reaching no conclusions. It is disappointing to see men who have a platform of unusual influence, and from whom a robust declaration of what matters and why it matters might have been expected, fudging their opportunity. Many hoped that more would be forthcoming upon further reflection, and that there would be some acknowledgements of failure and disappointment in addition to the pontifications about dichotomies and tensions. What happened? MacDonald resigned as a council member, to the warm commendations and hearty applause and well-wishing of several others. Mark Driscoll later stepped down from TGC council in the same way, enjoying a sort of spiritual golden handshake. With the lack of enduring concentration so typical of the blogosphere, the matter passed over quickly and has been largely forgotten. The problem is that what was required here was a thorough, substantial, explicit repudiation of error and those who proclaim it and—at the very least—a rebuke to and pursuit of repentance and restoration from those who were countenancing its proclamation. Instead, the silence was staggering. TGC—unelected, unanswerable to any but themselves, not a church, not a denomination, not much that can very easily be pinned down—essentially gave their imprimatur to some of this by a failure properly to censure it, and in so doing risked (and quite possibly achieved) a staggering and dangerous level of confusion and obfuscation among the many with whom their words (or lack of them) carry much weight. The absence of further and appropriate comment on this from TGC remains a genuine concern.

While the UK has, perhaps, yet to see anything of this magnitude, I am not the only observer to have concerns about the drive to build ever-bigger platforms and organisations and institutions, a drive which generally involves a necessary willingness to sacrifice truth that matters (whether considered primary or secondary). We are increasingly informed (or, in practice, shown) that certain matters once considered significant are now relegated to the matter of secondary truth, with the emphasis on secondary, the synonym for 'secondary' in this instance seeming to be 'negligible.' We see this downgrade, for example, in the area of ecclesiology (whether church nature, polity, government, or planting), in the matter of worship, in the nature of preaching, in the cultivation of holiness, in the attitude to the charismata (see below), and in a number of other areas.

I would suggest that this ecumenism is not that Scriptural communion and cooperation which any right-minded believer would pursue, but rather a watering down of that crisp and clear definition which serves the church of Christ best. It has become, in some instances, a dissolution of distinctiveness that will damage the church and her witness before the world. In short, there comes a clear point at which—whatever shipyard a vessel is from and whatever flag it may be flying—it is clearly a pirate and ought to be treated as such if the king's ships are going to retain any kind of credibility.

As stated earlier, unity and peace at the expense of truth and righteousness is a wicked and unconscionable trade-off. Those who dare to question or critique are often and quickly condemned, made to seem or feel profoundly unspiritual because this ecumenism has appropriated to itself a flag labelled 'gospel' under which to sail its flotilla of ships, and who dares to fire a shot across the bows of the lead vessel? Queries about the definition of this gospel, and what it ought to include and exclude, are dismissed as narrowness or vindictiveness, thoughtless carping in a day when greater things are afoot.

The complaints of those in the movement who have been subjected to criticism have sounded at times all too much like Ahab complaining that Elijah is a troubler of Israel, and the snake-oil that is being poured on troubled waters should not be allowed to still the storm of righteous indignation at a failure to expose heresy and censure heretics and those who harbour them (2 John 7–11). If these kinds of boundaries are considered negotiable, then there is something profoundly dangerous taking place which needs swiftly to be addressed.

Spiritual gifts

Furthermore, there is for many new Calvinists *a genuine tension with regard to spiritual gifts.* This has been identified even within the movement itself as a potential faultline, a point of division which could cause significant dissension. I think the men who have recognized that tension are right, but the present response is often to keep papering over the cracks even while some are driving in the wedges (please permit the tortured analogy). For many the issue of spiritual gifts and the nature of the continuing work of the

Spirit of Christ seems to be a moot point—it will not be addressed; it must be overlooked; it will not be allowed to become an issue. In a book in which a number of prominent confessional figures were interviewed (for not only the new Calvinists have their figureheads), some of whom are working within or on the fringes of this movement, the only contributor to those interviews who specifically suggested that the charismatic influence is a dangerous one was Conrad Mbewe, a Zambian pastor.[46] Almost no one else wanted to address the fact that this is and should be a point of genuine tension, a point of potential and actual divide.

This thoughtlessness or carelessness may be one of the lingering influences of the Emerging/Emergent church approach from which some new Calvinists have graduated. But the matter of spiritual gifts and activity is and ought to be recognised as a significant issue and it is something that is front and centre in new Calvinism. Mark Driscoll has described himself as 'a Charismatic wearing a seatbelt,' but testified to a significant development in his approach following substantial interaction with the Newfrontiers movement in the UK (including speaking at their flagship conference). Subsequently, Driscoll deeply grieved many by his assertion that he possesses a gift of discernment by means of which he sees visions of 'women raped. I've seen children molested. I've seen people abused. I've seen people beaten. I've seen horrible things done. Horrible things done. I've seen children dedicated in occultic groups and demons come upon them as an infant by invitation. And I wasn't present for any of it, but I've seen it visibly.'[47] Others, like C. J. Mahaney, have always been thoroughly and expansively Charismatic in their pneumatology, though often significantly more guarded than Mark Driscoll in their public pronouncements. John Piper explored the Vineyard movement to the extent of encouraging a number of the members of the church he serves to attend the Vineyard meetings while warning them not to get swept away,[48] and—though more guarded about the later Toronto Blessing—has not, as far as I know, formally repudiated what he found there. Wayne Grudem's *Systematic Theology* (IVP, 1994) (together with his more developed teaching in *The Gift of Prophecy* [Crossway, 1998, revised 2000]) has provided a scholarly justification for the expectation of continued apostolic gifts and especially 'prophetic words,' though we must remember that many practitioners are far less guarded than Grudem in their approach.[49]

Indeed, the matter is becoming more pressing. Mark Driscoll has suggested that the 'current global movement in Christianity' is characterized by four theological distinctives—Reformed theology, complementarian relationships, Spirit-filled lives, and missional churches.[50]

In the course of the same address Driscoll made the assertion that 'cessationism is worldliness,' what he characterised as a sort of rationalistic, modernistic, Cartesian, Humean scepticism with regard to the supernatural. (Another, more recent, popular snippet from Driscoll, taken from a sermon on Revelation 2:1–7, has him setting up a false dichotomy between doctrine and the immediate work of the Holy Spirit.[51]) John Piper has asserted via Twitter that 'God humbles Charismatics by making their children Calvinists; and Calvinists by making their children speak in tongues.'[52] Ahem!

This is pertinent especially in the UK and perhaps in other places. As previously mentioned, the new Calvinist spectrum in the US is a broad one. In other places it can appear narrower. In the UK, expressions of new Calvinism are often Charismatic or at least thoroughly ambivalent with regard to the matter of gifts, some of those expressions being centred in the Newfrontiers movement, who have enthusiastically bought into and endorsed (and benefited from the association with) the ministries of some of the big American names. This version of the new Calvinism is flowing out from these circles into others, often carrying with it those Charismatic emphases and all that usually goes with them, and the whole package is sometimes being thoughtlessly embraced by those who ought to know better. Where figureheads of the Charismatic movement have not been offered a specific opportunity for influence, numerous churches, local associations of churches, conferences and other gatherings have deliberately downplayed or overlooked this matter as being of no significance: again, the appearance of unity and the pursuit of bigness seem to trump all other considerations.

But who is this person, this Holy Spirit, and what does he do? How does he do what he does? When and in what ways does he do it? Is there any difference of nature or of degree between what he was doing in the days of the apostles and what he is doing now? There are some men within the new Calvinist movement who would, I think, be very close to a more orthodox Reformed perspective (a narrower spectrum), but I think the broad stream of new Calvinism is essentially a continuationist stream, sometimes extravagantly so.

I admit that I do not like being labelled a cessationist, because of the implications that language often carries. I do not believe, in any absolute sense, that the Holy Spirit has stopped working. Christians depend upon him entirely, in every moment of our living, our serving, our worshipping. He is the One by whom Christ is made known to us and through whom we enter into and experience and enjoy our union with the risen Lord. We do not want to be driven into a corner where we become so worried about abuses regarding the Holy Spirit that we give him up. If we do so, we would become absolute cessationists, and that would be blasphemous. Some of us are in danger of knowing all that the Holy Spirit does not do, and ignoring or forgetting or fearing much or all of what he does. We are in danger of saying, or of seeming to say, 'We are so worried about abuses regarding the Holy Spirit, we will relinquish him altogether. You Charismatics may have him. We will be absolute cessationists and you will be the continuationists.' That is a caricature of Reformed orthodoxy that we must not embrace. But all of us must answer the questions: What is the nature of his work? What is the nature, extent and degree of his work in times past, present and future? Are we to expect prophecies, healings, miracles in what are (at least in some eyes) post-apostolic times? These questions and honest answers to them must necessarily have significant effects upon our polity and practice as churches, individually and together.

When people gather at some of the big new Calvinist conferences, some of these issues get put aside. Everybody gets together and gives the impression of a quite complete unity (ironing over a few choppy patches during some of the singing, perhaps—to stay safe, sit on the front row and don't look behind you). But what happens when everybody goes back to their individual churches? At that level there are radical and significant differences in approach to these things. Ultimately, though, this is not just about whether or not one church believes in prophetic utterances and speaking in unknown or angelic tongues, but with the whole nature of authority in its relation to divine revelation. Where does God speak to us? How does he make his will known today? That has become and must be a flashpoint. It is another place in which many have a strong desire to hold together things that simply do not belong together, and not just in man's opinion. You will hear the phrase 'Reformed Charismatic.' Some would suggest, with credibility, that those two things are mutually exclusive, precisely because of this issue of authority and revelation. The questions surely arise, which of those two influences is going to take the ascendancy in the movement, and what will be the outcome?

Triumphalism

My sixth concern is with what I perceive as *a degree of arrogance and triumphalism* in some new Calvinists. I make this statement as one exceedingly conscious that I am prone to the same spirit, but—while recognizing my own frailties in this area—let me suggest more specifically what I mean. This is a young, though now maturing, and seemingly successful movement. What tends to happen when you are young and successful?

Often you get a big head and you think that you must be right and you just need to keep going and that everyone and everything will eventually fall before you. I fear a developing—and, in some, a developed—sense of being above contradiction, that they have it made, and that the movement will continue to roll over all that stands in its way. This is true especially of some of those who are coming in around and just behind some of the figureheads. You can read assertions from fairly prominent individuals that in the past something similar to this movement has happened, but it all fell apart … but this time it's different, this time it's better, this time we've got it right, this time it's here to stay, this time it will last, this time the onward march will not falter.

Such triumphalism can quickly breed overconfidence, even brashness. For example, bombastic pronunciations about targets reached in church-planting programmes (without much long-term demonstration of the enduring validity and health of those churches) are par for the course. At times you will hear men speaking as if they have just reinvented the wheel. For example, one treatment of the church was introduced with the staggering assertion that there has not been a serious consideration of the issue since the days of the Protestant Reformation, the implication being that the gap was about to be plugged. Now if that isn't a dose

of hubristic nonsense, kindly fax me an explanation of
what is! Readers will, I hope, not be surprised to learn
that there are, in fact, one or two books dealing with
ecclesiology written since the Reformation. Could it be
that our author simply failed to read them? Again, it
goes along with the enthusiasm of the movement: 'Hey,
look! I am just discovering these things!' 'That's great,'
we respond, 'but so have other people.' 'I've discovered
Edwards,' says one, 'let me tell you what Edwards says!'
'That's wonderful!' we reply, 'but other people have been
reading Edwards before you and with you and they also
have some valid perspectives on what Edwards says.'
Some of these areas or interpretations of theology have
simply been co-opted by the new Calvinists. It is seen
in their handling of history; I think at times they can
give the impression that if you just read history properly
you will see that it vindicates the new Calvinism. This
is not an isolated problem, and certainly not one from
which others are immune. When we read history, what
we tend to find (or, at least, to see) are the examples
that suggest to us that we are doing the right thing right
now, and so we vindicate ourselves: in our own reading,
history proves that we are right. While it is not wrong to
approach history from a point of prior conviction, and
I would suggest in many cases it is right and necessary,
this approach can too easily become an illegitimate way
of handling the past.

Alongside of this is a tendency only to dialogue and receive criticism within one's own relatively closed circle. New Calvinists seem to talk to each other, even about each other, they interact readily with each other, but if you are someone who has been judged or placed 'outside' for some reason, and you have the temerity to suggest that one of the figureheads may have something wrong, then woe betide! Again, as an example, a fairly typical response to the Elephant Room 2 debacle involved the rebuke that since those on the outside could not possibly be privy to the discussions taking place among the key figures on the inside, those on the outside ought simply to hold their tongues and make no assessments and offer no critiques. There are some blogs and other sites where critical comments are quickly excised, as if dissenting voices are to be excluded from the conversation.

But the issue should not be whether something seems to be working or failing, whether it is big or small, or if one of the big dogs is barking. The issue is whether it is right or wrong. I do think that there are times at which the sense that this movement is young and vigorous and moving—really going places, and fast—can blind some to inherent and developing weaknesses and can close the ears of some within to those of us who have been put without, but who desire their good and believe we have something to offer them at least as much as they have something to offer us. And there is evidence that under pressure from the belief in the virtue of bigness, the weight of numbers, and the sense of rapid progress, this arrogance may harden in some into a pride that refuses to be replied to, resisted or rebuked, and that would be a tragedy.

Summary

New Calvinism, *at its worst*, can seem or even be thoroughly man-centred. In various ways and at particular points it panders too much to the world, to the fallen culture, to the academy. There are sometimes prominent indications of concern for human approval, reliance on worldly means and principles, embrace of worldly models, and subsequent departure from or woolliness on historic orthodox Christianity at various important points. These features make some manifestations of new Calvinism a matter of concern and other manifestations a matter of outright danger.

There are some men and groups within the movement who are proving no safe spiritual guides, and there are too many who are silent about this when they ought to be speaking, with some bright and thoroughly commendable exceptions. Those within who are willing to speak and stand for the truth when it is assaulted need our prayers. Those who are drifting toward confusion or peddling error, wittingly or unwittingly, need prayer just as much, if not more.

The apparent speed and success of new Calvinism can be enticing. The fact that it can, in its various forms, and at different points along the spectrum, contain more or less that is wholesome alongside some of these departures and aberrations means that much discernment is required. On the one hand, we must not throw the baby out with the bathwater; on the other hand, if the baby has swallowed all the bathwater, we may not have a great deal of choice.

Chapter 5
Conclusions and counsels

What, then, are we to make of all this? How should we respond to the challenges and opportunities, the beauties over which we must rejoice and the confusions over which we might tremble?

My conclusion essentially is this: be Calvinists. Don't be new Calvinists or any other particular brand or stripe of Calvinists, whatever those distinctions may presently mean, or may come to mean. Fundamentally, I would urge you to live before God rather than before men. This means that we should consider what it means to serve the Lord in our particular circumstances and follow that course humbly and faithfully, individually and corporately, regardless of the pleasures or pains which that course seems to hold out.

With regard to the new Calvinism, we should avoid knee-jerk reactions, thoughtlessly dismissing or embracing something or someone, or everything and everyone, without proper consideration. In addition, we should avoid blanket judgments: the spectrum is too broad and the distinctions along it too fine to tar with the same brush every man or woman who takes or is given the label 'new Calvinist.' We need to show discernment as believers. That is true when someone calls themselves Reformed, an evangelical, or indeed a Calvinist—we would graciously ask what they mean by that, seeking to discover how much or how little we have in common, and to what extent we share common aims and might work together toward common goals. In the same way, we should give any man credibly claiming to be a brother in the Lord the opportunity to show his mettle.

So you do not need to capitulate to the immediate and ride the current of the moment. There is no need to join the convoy just because it is going past at speed, glowing with the power of the newest technology and applauded by adoring fans. Neither do you need to panic and send out warning signals, eminently suspicious of everyone who may not be 'one of us.' You do not need to shoot on sight, presuming that every vessel from the new Calvinist shipyard is sailing under an enemy flag, or—still worse—the skull-and-crossbones.

Take each case on its merit: we may not always agree with a genuine spiritual brother at all points, and we may have significant disagreement with those whom we love in the Lord. However, we should remember that—until their doctrine or practice prove otherwise—we are to behave with sincere affection and a proper humility toward those who are brothers and sisters in Christ, and should treat them as such in all respects *until* their doctrine or practice prove that they are otherwise. At that point we should set out to recover them from their errors (2 Timothy 2:24–26) by all appropriate and legitimate means. If they are genuine brothers and sisters with whom we genuinely and sincerely disagree, then we should acknowledge that there is a righteous way to respond in cultivating our own humility and faithfulness, maintaining an appropriate relationship, resisting any confusion and error, and offering direction and encouragement toward the truth. Of course, and as we have already said, neither can we forget that there is nothing loving about overlooking deceit and ignoring wickedness:

This is love, that we walk according to His commandments. This is the commandment, that as you have heard from the beginning, you should walk in it. For many deceivers have gone out into the world who do not confess Jesus Christ as coming in the flesh. This is a deceiver and an antichrist. Look to yourselves, that we do not lose those things we worked for, but that we may receive a full reward. Whoever transgresses and does not abide in the doctrine of Christ does not have God. He who abides in the doctrine of Christ has both the Father and the Son. If anyone comes to you and does not bring this doctrine, do not receive him into your house nor greet him; for he who greets him shares in his evil deeds. (2 John 6–11)

We must be Calvinists. We must recognize and remember that we are united in Christ with all true believers, although we do have differences of opinion, some of them significant. God is their Father and our Father, and he is in control of all things for the glory of his name and the good of all his redeemed people. None of Christ's will be lost. The purposes of our heavenly Father are being accomplished in the earth. His kingdom is advancing. Our responsibility is to live before God to the praise of his glory.

Some of us—and I put myself firmly in this category—ought to get on with the business of making Christ known and serving those whom he calls where he has put us. We are not called, first and foremost, to spend all our time worrying about other shepherds, but more to give ourselves to following the Great Shepherd in our convictions and actions. We must look first to ourselves in this regard and ensure that our doctrine and our practice marry, that we manifest degrees of heat and of light that are coordinate with and complementary to one another. We neither know all we should, nor do all that we know, and it is in the equal march of faith and life, knowing and doing, telling and showing, that we gain the platform that will enable us to serve our friends who differ from us in other respects.

C. H. Spurgeon, speaking in his lecture on the Wesley brothers of the attitude of some toward those holy men, said,

> I am afraid that most of us are half-asleep and those that are a little awake have not begun to feel. It will be time for us to find fault with John and Charles Wesley, not when we discover their mistakes, but when we have cured our own. When we shall have more piety than they, more fire than they, more grace, more burning love, more intense unselfishness, then, and not till then, may we begin to find fault and criticize.[53]

I can sincerely say that it is in this spirit that I have written. Our first responsibility is to set our own house in order, and to set out to live in accordance with the light we have received, stirring up the fires of grace and piety and holy endeavour. If we can learn from those whose faith and love and hope exceed ours, then we should not be too proud to do so.

But be Calvinists. I presume that you believe what you believe because you actually believe it and believe that it matters to believe it, and not because you have simply inherited it or assumed it. You have, I trust, thought through your convictions. You have searched the Scriptures to see whether the things you have learned from godly men are true, and you have anchored yourself at certain points of doctrine and their corresponding practice because you are persuaded that those things are true and right before God and that you will live accordingly.

If we have done this with a good conscience, then we should hold fast to our convictions and live them out to the praise and the glory of God. Enjoy these things! Enter into the sweet realities of the God that we know in his Son, Jesus Christ, and in communion with the Holy Spirit, and graciously defend the truths you have come to love and the practices that flow from the principles. You are not obliged to give them up any more than our new Calvinist brothers are obliged to give things up just because we disagree with them. There is and should be scope for us to speak together as those who love the Lord: 'To the law and to the testimony!' should be our sincere cry. Let us be ready both to learn with humility where we have something to learn and to teach with modesty where we have something to teach.

From its beginning, the new Calvinism was in some respects a splendid and many-coloured thing. But it did have and still does involve some fearful tensions. It has within it still some wonderful prospects and it contains within it some significant and increasingly evident dangers. But remember that mere fads never last. I am far from saying that the new Calvinism is a mere fad, but there is an appetite for novelty in the world and among professing Christians that has carried and perhaps is still carrying people into this movement on a wave of enthusiasm. The novelty will not last forever and the freshness is already fading, despite what will be the increasingly desperate attempts of some to keep the fireworks going off by increasingly extreme gestures and gimmicks.

I suspect that when the freshness and the newness wears off, we will be left with many people asking at least two questions. Some will say, and are already saying, 'What next?' They will look for the next fad, the next new wave, and will jump aboard and be carried on to whatever seems new and stimulating. But some will ask, and are already asking, 'What more? What else is there? What am I missing? This is the God that I want to know and serve. How can I know him more? How can I know him better without losing that sense of wonder because of God's love and grace toward me in Christ Jesus? How can I grow in the grace and knowledge of our Lord and Saviour Jesus Christ? How can I grow in holiness, becoming more and more like Christ Jesus?'

We need so to live and so to speak that when somebody asks, 'What more?' we have a reputation and a relationship that enable us credibly to hold something out, to offer with humble joy the blessings that we have received, just as much as we receive with humble joy whatever blessings we may be offered.

Such a stance requires at least two anchor points: the truth of Scripture and the church of Christ. An intelligent and wholehearted commitment to a more comprehensive, tried-and-tested expression of Scriptural truth provides a buffer against the kind of shocks that drive men and churches off their feet. I admit that adherence to an historic and full-orbed confession of faith (rather than a minimal outline of truth) is not a panacea, as history proves. I am not putting confessions on a par with the Word of God, and I accept that all confessions are, in measure, of their time and circumstances: there is as much a danger that writing new ones will make us slaves of the present as that embracing old ones will lock us into the past. Nevertheless, we need to set our feet upon a doctrinal rock where others have proved that a saint can safely stand when buffeted by the winds and waves of falsehood. The preparation for the downgrade of Spurgeon's day was made by those men who resisted a more complete and binding declaration of the things clearly expressed in and surely believed from the Bible, and who settled instead for a sort of gentleman's agreement on those nebulous things described as 'the sentiments usually denominated evangelical.'[54]

In addition, we need to operate within the Scripturally-appointed bounds of the local, visible church. I appreciate that some who might agree with substantial portions of my critique and even this portion of my response will differ from me on the precise nature of the church and on the nature of its relationship to parachurch ministries and organisations. Nevertheless, I hope that many will agree with me on this: that it is within the orbit of the local congregation under the care of spiritually qualified, identifiably competent and genuinely accountable men that the saints will best grow in the grace and knowledge of Jesus Christ. The surest foundation for present and future faithfulness and fruitfulness will be a robustly confessional ecclesiology, a well-grounded churchmanship not subject to the currents of the age or the whims of the demagogues. Standing and serving on such a basis and in such an environment will best equip the church to be a blessing to the world in which we live and to others whom we hope to help.

So be Calvinists. Do not panic blindly. Do not capitulate foolishly. Do not strike wildly. Live before God and be determined to learn of Christ in dependence on the Holy Spirit. Love and serve the triune God above all, and be ready to love and serve his saints wherever you find them, and however your supreme attachment to the Lord of glory demands it.

Individuals of Note

Voddie Baucham is a pastor at Grace Family Baptist Church in Spring, Texas, and also wears hats as an author, professor, conference speaker and church planter.

Don Carson is currently Research Professor at Trinity Evangelical Divinity School in Chicago, Illinois (where he has served since 1978), before which he was a pastor for three years in Richmond, British Columbia, in his native Canada, and tutor and dean at Northwest Baptist Theological College and Seminary. He is co-founder, with Tim Keller, of The Gospel Coalition, and is also a voluminous author and well-travelled speaker.

Tim Challies is a pastor of Grace Fellowship Church, Toronto, Canada. He is a writer, best known as the founder and proprietor of Challies.com, probably the pre-eminent blog of the new Calvinist movement. He is also editor of the Discerning Reader website and a co-founder of Cruciform Press.

Francis Chan is the former pastor of Cornerstone Community Church in Simi Valley, California, the founder and Chancellor of Eternity Bible College and author of several books, including the best-selling *Crazy Love*. He resigned from his pastorate in April 2010 and his website now states that he is 'working to start a church planting movement in the inner city of San Francisco and also working to launch a countrywide discipleship movement.'

Matt Chandler is lead pastor of teaching at The Village Church of Dallas, Fort Worth, having pastored there since 2002, since when church attendance has increased from 160 people to over 10,000. He is also president of the Acts 29 Network. He has co-authored *The Explicit Gospel* and *Creature of the Word*.

Tim Chester is a pastor and church planter with The Crowded House, is co-founder and associate director of the Porterbrook Seminary. He has authored a number of books. He has recently joined the faculty of the Wales Evangelical School of Theology.

Mark Dever has been the senior pastor of the Capitol Hill Baptist Church in Washington, D.C. since 1994. He is author of a number of books and is the president of 9Marks, a ministry intended to promote the establishment of biblically faithful churches.

Mark Driscoll is founder and current preaching pastor of Mars Hill Church in Seattle, Washington, co-founder of Churches Helping Churches and the Acts 29 Network, of which he served as president until that role passed to Matt Chandler. His church website describes him as 'one of the world's most downloaded and quoted pastors.' He travels widely, and is a fairly prolific blogger and author.

Kevin DeYoung is the senior pastor at University Reformed Church (a Reformed Church in America congregation) in East Lansing, Michigan, near Michigan State University. He has authored a number of books, including (with Ted Kluck) *Why We're Not Emergent* and *Why We Love the Church*, as well as being a highly-regarded blogger.

Ligon Duncan is pastor of First Presbyterian Church (Presbyterian Church in America), Jackson, Mississippi. He is currently president of the Alliance of Confessing Evangelicals, as well as a council member of The Gospel Coalition.

Steven Furtick is the founder and lead pastor of Elevation Church in Charlotte, North Carolina, and is the author of the books *Sun Stand Still* and *Greater*.

Wayne Grudem is currently research professor of Theology and Biblical Studies at Phoenix Seminary, Arizona, before which he taught for twenty years at Trinity Evangelical Divinity School. He has written a number of influential books, and co-founded the Council on biblical Manhood and Womanhood, as well as serving as the general editor of the *ESV Study Bible*.

Tim Keller is the founding pastor of Redeemer Presbyterian Church in Manhattan, New York, and chairman of Redeemer City to City, a church planting organisation. He is a best-selling author, well-known apologist and popular speaker; he teaches at Westminster Seminary, Philadelphia, Pennsylvania, and is co-founder of The Gospel Coalition, alongside Don Carson.

Tope Koleoso is the lead pastor for 'preaching and vision' of Jubilee Church, Enfield, London. Jubilee Church is a Newfrontiers church.

John MacArthur, Jr. is pastor-teacher of Grace Community Church in Sun Valley, California, a popular author, conference speaker, and broadcaster. He is also the president of The Master's College and The Master's Seminary.

James MacDonald is the founder and senior pastor of Harvest Bible Chapel, a multi-campus church in and around Chicago, Illinois. He is a broadcaster and author. He is 'curator' of The Elephant Room.

C. J. Mahaney is currently the senior pastor of Sovereign Grace Church of Louisville. Until recently, he was also president of Sovereign Grace Ministries (formerly People of Destiny International or PDI), a network formed to establish and support local churches, and was one of the founding pastors and leaders of Covenant Life Church in Gaithersburg, Maryland.

Conrad Mbewe is pastor of Lusaka Baptist Church, Zambia, a well-travelled preacher and a blogger.

R. Albert Mohler, Jr. is the current president of Southern Baptist Theological Seminary in Louisville, Kentucky. Mohler is a theologian and author of note.

Perry Noble is the founder and senior pastor of NewSpring Church, a multi-campus church in South Carolina.

Ray Ortlund, Jr. is pastor of Immanuel Church in Nashville, TN, president of Renewal Ministries, a regional director in the Acts 29 Network, and a council member of and blogger at The Gospel Coalition.

John Piper served as Pastor for Preaching and Vision at Bethlehem Baptist Church in Minneapolis, Minnesota, from 1980 until March 2013, when he retired from pastoral ministry. He is founder of Desiring God Ministries, named after his seminal volume, *Desiring God: Meditations of a Christian Hedonist.* He has authored numerous other volumes.

R. C. Sproul, Sr. is co-pastor of Saint Andrew's Chapel in Sanford, Florida, chairman of Ligonier Ministries, and president of Reformation Bible College. He is well known as a preacher, teacher, broadcaster and writer.

Jonathan Stephen, following a brief career in teaching, was a pastor at Amyand Park Chapel, Twickenham, London, and then at Carey Baptist Church, Reading. He is a past president of the FIEC and Director of Affinity, and became principal at Wales Evangelical School of Theology in 2006.

Justin Taylor is an elder at New Covenant Bible Church in St Charles, Illinois, and vice president of book publishing and an associate publisher at Crossway, before which he worked at Desiring God. He blogs at Between Two Worlds and has edited and contributed to several books.

Steve Timmis is co-founder of The Crowded House church(es), and the co-director of the Porterbrook Network, training church planters. He is the director of Acts 29 in Western Europe and has recently joined the faculty of the Wales Evangelical School of Theology.

Terry Virgo is based at Kings Church, Kingston, London, and is the founder of the Newfrontiers family of charismatic churches. He has been given preaching and teaching opportunities through or at—among others, UCCF, the FIEC and New Word Alive.

Adrian Warnock is part of the leadership team of

Jubilee Church, Enfield, London, and now blogs under the Patheos banner.

Rick Warren is the founder and senior pastor of Saddleback Church in Lake Forest, California. He is probably best known for his two books, *The Purpose Driven Church* and *The Purpose Driven Life*.

Douglas Wilson is pastor at Christ Church in Moscow, Idaho, faculty member at New Saint Andrews College, a prolific author and popular speaker. He is regularly cited as a key figure in the movement known as the Federal Vision (also called hyper-covenantalism).

Notes

1   B. B. Warfield, *Works* (Grand Rapids, MI: Baker, 1991), 5:354–5.

2   Bearing in mind that the five points have not always been identified or defined in precisely the same way by orthodox Calvinists down through the years, and are a relatively recent phenomenon.

3   Of course, just as not all new Calvinists are Amyraldians, neither are all Amyraldians new Calvinists. There is simply some overlap between the two groups at this point of doctrine.

4   MacArthur has delivered a series of quite vigorous addresses to the 'young, restless and reformed' crowd, and several of his points were very poorly received, in the main, although some gave a more seasoned and dignified response. His vocal cessationist stance also tends to alienate him from them.

5   The story is related in Andrew Fuller, ed. Andrew Gunton Fuller, *Complete Works* (Harrisonburg, VA: Sprinkle Publications,1988), 1:111. It should be obvious that this is not a danger restricted to the new Calvinism.

6   Stephen's undated (1990s?) pamphlet, *Bible Churches Together: A Plea for True Ecumenism*, shows several emphases in common with what is now called new Calvinism, emphases still evident in the FIEC and Affinity. Recent alliances that WEST has made with, for example, Acts 29 and the Porterbrook Network reveal if not an entire agreement then at the very least an earnest sympathy with others in the new Calvinist sphere.

7   *1689 (Second London) Baptist Confession of Faith*, 26:14.

8   Don Carson and Tim Keller insist upon this language with

regard to The Gospel Coalition at http://thegospelcoalition.org/blogs/
tgc/2011/10/11/reflections-on-confessionalism-boundaries-and-discipline/,
accessed Thu. 18 Jul 13.

9   For example, The Gospel Coalition's foundation documents can be
accessed at http://thegospelcoalition.org/about/who.

10   Heath Lambert provides a telling review of this volume at http://
www.dennyburk.com/wp-content/uploads/2012/04/8-Lambert.pdf

11   Originally viewed at http://www.youtube.com/watch?v=
1RE4iu97Ryw. The video has now been taken out of the public space.

12   Mark Driscoll, *Confessions of a Reformission Rev* (Grand Rapids,
MI: Zondervan, 2006), 28.

13   See http://www.time.com/time/specials/packages/
article/0,28804,1884779_1884782_1884760,00.html, accessed 20 Sep 11.

14   http://bigstory.ap.org/article/first-amendment-defense-signaled-
sex-abuse-case accessed Tues. 05 Mar 13.

15   D. Martyn Lloyd-Jones, *Setting Our Affections Upon Glory: Nine
Sermons on the Gospel and the Church* (Wheaton, IL: Crossway, 2013), 110.

16   http://thegospelcoalition.org/blogs/tgc/2013/01/28/driscoll-who-do-
you-think-i-am/, accessed Tues. 05 Feb 13.

17   http://www.reformation21.org/articles/the-nameless-one.php,
accessed Wed. 06 Feb 13.

18   Quoted in James D. Bratt (ed.), *Abraham Kuyper: A Centennial
Reader* (Grand Rapids, MI: Eerdmans, 1998), 488.

19   Though this is found most readily in men like Andy Stanley
(senior pastor of North Point Community Church, Buckhead Church,
Browns Bridge Community Church, Gwinnett Church and Watermarke
Church—all at once, apparently), who would perhaps not fit readily within
the parameters of the new Calvinism, this has become common parlance
among many new Calvinists. For a more mainstream statement, consider
something like http://thegospelcoalition.org/blogs/trevinwax/2007/08/29/
why-you-should-love-god-with-your-mind/, accessed Tues. 23 Jul 13. The
language, and the dismissal of the distinction, is common.

20   This seems to be the approach of David Green in his Affinity Table
Talk paper, which contains arguments that I would say are typical of the
new Calvinist approach to culture at this point. The paper can be found at

http://www.affinity.org.uk/downloads/Table%20Talk/Table-Talk-2013.1-Generational-Differences-in-Church.pdf, accessed Fri. 01 Feb 13.

21   See, for example, some sections of Tim Keller's *The Reason for God*, which—depending on who you ask—either falls into the void of the achingly hip or stands as the paradigm for relevant communication.

22   Their articles on the regulative principle can be seen at http://www.9marks.org/search/node/regulative%20principle, accessed Thu. 18 Jul 13.

23   http://www.9marks.org/blog/what-about-movie-clips-applying-regulative-principle, accessed Thu. 18 Jul 13

24   See, for example, http://www.desiringgod.org/resource-library/sermons/all-of-life-as-worship, or the Newfrontiers-influenced website http://confluenceblog.com/all-life-is-worship, or Darrin Patrick at http://www.youtube.com/watch?v=6T4re5dcEq8, all accessed Tues. 23 Jul 13.

25   In case that reference passes you by, it refers usually to younger people who embrace independent rather than mainstream or allegedly more commercial expressions of culture, usually in the realm of the arts. The same principle of adaptation works whichever subsection of community and culture you are interested in reaching. If you needed that explained, there are those who might conclude that you are, indeed, beyond hope!

26   Tim Keller, *The Reason for God: Belief in an Age of Skepticism* (New York, NY: Dutton, 2008), 192.

27   http://biologos.org/about, accessed Wed. 26 Jun 13.

28   http://biologos.org, accessed Wed. 26 Jun 13.

29   A fourteen page document available at http://biologos.org/uploads/projects/Keller_white_paper.pdf, accessed Wed. 26 Jun 13, which sets out Keller's views more fully.

30   http://biologos.org/uploads/projects/Keller_white_paper.pdf, accessed Wed. 26 Jun 13, page 13.

31   For a more detailed discussion of many of these points, see Iain D. Campbell and William M. Schweitzer (eds.), *Engaging With Keller: Thinking Through the Theology of an Influential Evangelical* (Darlington, UK: Evangelical Press, 2013).

32   For a British but typical approach to this matter, see John Steven's essay on 'Why Easter means I'm not a sabbatarian' at http://www.john-

stevens.com/2012/04/theology-why-easter-means-im-not.html, accessed Tues. 23 Jul 13. For fairness in critique, interested readers should also consider John Steven's survey of the law in Deuteronomy, beginning here http://www.john-stevens.com/2013/06/the-law-in-deuteronomy-how-does-law.html, accessed Tue 23 Jul 13.

33   For a typical expression of this, see Tom Schreiner's *40 Questions About Christians and biblical Law* (Kregel, 2010); an excerpt concerning the Fourth Commandment can be found at http://thegospelcoalition.org/blogs/justintaylor/2010/10/14/schreiner-qa-is-the-sabbath-still-required-for-christians/, accessed Thu. 18 Jul 13.

34   J. C. Ryland Jr. 'Preface to the Second London Edition' in Robert Hall, ed. Nathan A. Finn, *Help to Zion's Travellers* (Mountain Home, AR: Borderstone Press, 2011), lii. Ryland's extended comments on this matter are well worth reading.

35   See, for example, his *The Hole in our Holiness* (Crossway, 2012).

36   See, for example, his *Jesus + Nothing = Everything* (Crossway, 2011).

37   See, for example, http://www.desiringgod.org/blog/posts/kevin-deyoung-and-john-piper-discuss-the-pursuit-of-holiness-part-1, accessed Thu. 11 Jul 13.

38   Grammatically, the indicative mood is used to express simple statement of facts. So, gospel indicatives are the established realities of underlying gospel truth, rooted in God's sovereign and gracious acts.

39   Grammatically, the imperative mood is used to express commands or exhortations. Thus, gospel imperatives are those commands or exhortations that come to Christians as believers and which, vitally, rely on gospel indicatives to give them their force and substance. Typically, the relation between the indicative and the imperative would be 'because … therefore …'

40   http://www.desiringgod.org/blog/posts/john-piper-interviews-rick-warren-on-doctrine, accessed Mon. 19 Aug 13. A helpful response from within the same circles can be found at http://www.challies.com/articles/thinking-about-rick-warren-john-piper, accessed Mon. 19 Aug 13. For a more rigorous assessment of the invitation rather than the interview, see http://teampyro.blogspot.co.uk/2010/04/on-piper-warren-connection.html, also accessed on Mon. 19 Aug 13.

41   Though it should be noted that in an interview with Rick Warren,

John Piper went beyond this and seemed to give him a substantial pass in pretty much all areas.

42   https://www.youtube.com/watch?v=2wNuxEonrog. The video has since been classified as private. However, a more detailed discussion of the sequence can be found at http://teampyro.blogspot.co.uk/2011/09/highway-to-hell.html, accessed Wed. 17 Sep 13.

43   Also called Sabellianism, this heresy denies the Trinity. Rather than acknowledging three persons—Father, Son and Spirit—within the Godhead, modalism presents instead the idea of a monadic God in three modes or aspects.

44   Tom Chantry's transcript of the session can be found at http://apprising.org/2012/02/02/t-d-jakes-in-the-elephant-room-ii-session-4-transcript/, accessed Thu. 11 Jul 13.

45   http://thegospelcoalition.org/blogs/tgc/2012/02/03/carson-and-keller-on-jakes-and-the-elephant-room/.

46   A typical recent piece from Pastor Mbewe is http://www.conradmbewe.com/2013/07/why-is-charismatic-movement-thriving-in.html, accessed Tue 23 Jul 13. I mean to level no snide accusations at Pastor Mbewe, a man whom I highly esteem, when I acknowledge that in none of these articles, so far as I am aware, does he address the issue of whether or how the African charismatic excesses against which he protests differ from the charismatic belief and practice of some American evangelicals with whom he seems happier to cooperate. I imagine that he would class some of the latter as more like the 'old-school Pentecostals,' more conservative and more deeply rooted in Scripture. In personal correspondence he also made the distinction between his personal and plainly-stated conviction worked out in his own life and in the local church, and temporary cooperation in an environment in which he is still free to hold and express his own views (*e.g.* at a conference) with those who share a broader agreement but differ on this matter. I will leave others to debate whether or not this is an appropriate 'degree of separation'!

47   Phil Johnson provides a transcript and commentary at http://teampyro.blogspot.co.uk/2011/08/pornographic-divination.html.

48   http://matthiasmedia.com/briefing/2011/10/a-conversation-with-john-piper/, accessed Thu. 11 Jul 13.

49   Those interested in a response to Grudem on this matter are encouraged to watch the discussion which took place between Grudem

and Ian Hamilton of Cambridge Presbyterian Church at the Evangelical Ministers Assembly 2010, available at http://vimeo.com/37169587.

50   http://theresurgence.com/2011/07/25/four-points-of-the-movement, accessed 20 Sep 11.

51   http://www.youtube.com/watch?v=XUXfHaHUkvo, accessed 23 May 12.

52   http://twitter.com/#!/JohnPiper/status/108222441356136449, posted on 29 Aug 11.

53   Charles Spurgeon, *The Two Wesleys* (Pasadena, TX: Pilgrim Publications, 1975). We might further point out that Spurgeon went on to say that he did not find the Wesley 'fan-boys' (to use a modern phrase) uniformly pleasing, which we all might bear in mind about our particular heroes: 'Unless you can give him constant adulation, unless you are prepared to affirm that he had no faults, and that he had every virtue, even impossible virtues, you cannot possibly satisfy his admirers.'

54   E. A. Payne, *The Baptist Union: A Short History* (London: The Baptist Union of Great Britain and Ireland, 1982), 61.